Prompting Deeper Discussions

Prompting Deeper Discussions

A Teacher's Guide to Crafting Great Questions

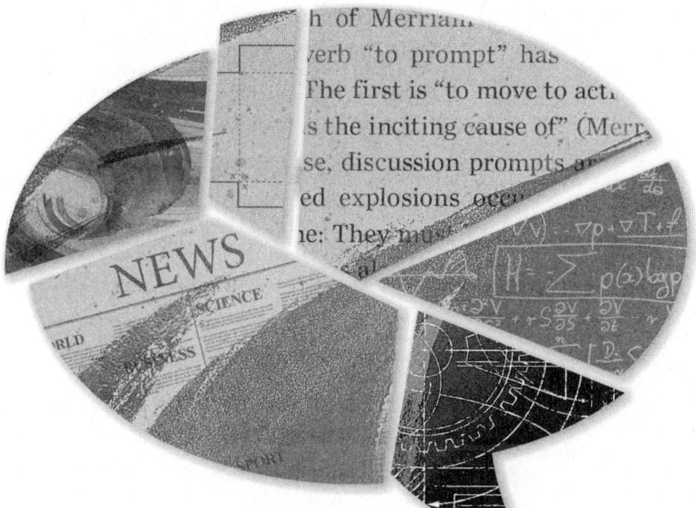

Matthew R. Kay

ascd
Arlington, Virginia USA

ascd

2800 Shirlington Road, Suite 1001 • Arlington, VA 22206 USA
Phone: 800-933-2723 or 703-578-9600
Website: www.ascd.org • Email: member@ascd.org
Author guidelines: www.ascd.org/write

Richard Culatta, *Chief Executive Officer;* Anthony Rebora, *Chief Content Officer;* Genny Ostertag, *Managing Director, Book Acquisitions & Editing;* Bill Varner, *Senior Acquisitions Editor;* Mary Beth Nielsen, *Director, Book Editing;* Liz Wegner, *Editor;* Catherine Gillespie, *Graphic Designer;* Valerie Younkin, *Senior Production Designer;* Kelly Marshall, *Production Manager;* Shajuan Martin, *E-Publishing Specialist;* Christopher Logan, *Senior Production Specialist;* Kathryn Oliver, *Creative Project Manager*

PAPERBACK ISBN: 978-1-4166-3339-6 ASCD product #124031 n12/24
PDF EBOOK ISBN: 978-1-4166-3340-2; see Books in Print for other formats.
Quantity discounts are available: email programteam@ascd.org or call 800-933-2723, ext. 5773, or 703-575-5773. For desk copies, go to www.ascd.org/deskcopy.

Library of Congress Cataloging-in-Publication Data
Names: Kay, Matthew R., 1983- author.
Title: Prompting deeper discussions : a teacher's guide to crafting great questions / Matthew R. Kay.
Description: Arlington, Virginia : ASCD, 2024. | Includes bibliographical references and index.
Identifiers: LCCN 2024036370 (print) | LCCN 2024036371 (ebook) | ISBN 9781416633396 (paperback) | ISBN 9781416633402 (pdf)
Subjects: LCSH: Discussion—Study and teaching—Activity programs. | Prompting (Education)—Study and teaching. | Group facilitation.
Classification: LCC LC6519 .K38 2024 (print) | LCC LC6519 (ebook) | DDC 371.3/7—dc23/eng/20240916
LC record available at https://lccn.loc.gov/2024036370
LC ebook record available at https://lccn.loc.gov/2024036371

34 33 32 31 30 29 28 27 26 25 1 2 3 4 5 6 7 8 9 10 11 12

In Loving Memory of Sherrill Jones Kay,
my mother, a 36-year teaching veteran,
and the reason I do what I do.

2/12/80 by R.C.Kay III

Prompting Deeper Discussions

A Teacher's Guide to Crafting Great Questions

Introduction: We Got to the Future *Fast*, Didn't We?

During my student teaching, my hands got chalky as I scribbled grammar rules on an old-school blackboard. At my first teaching job in 2005, I still faithfully used a physical grade book, like teachers had done for generations before me. Over time, a more robust internet, together with smartphones and more ubiquitous social media, showed up to radically change a lot of what teaching looked like. But with each shift, educators found a new equilibrium, as we always seem to do. Now, in a dizzying flash, we have all arrived at another radical change—one that we knew would one day exist, but only in some far-off *Star Trek* future: the dazzling era of generative AI. Suddenly, our students can access digital clerks that can craft everything for them, from essays and stories to music, artwork, and "original" films. And even *more* advanced versions of these AI tools will be around to help these students when they are adults, "writing" not only their grant proposals and expense reports, but also the wedding vows that make future partners weep.

I cannot name all the ways that these rapid technological advancements might influence our classroom instruction. I *can* say, with a certainty that is rare to come by nowadays, that if we teachers don't know how to lead a high-quality class discussion about a book, time period, or a scientific or mathematical theory, this deficit will hurt more than it ever has. Because from now until forever, our students will know that every book, time period, or theory can be broken down and analyzed for them, then processed into any artifact they want.

So—wildly—if students don't want to go through the productive struggle of creating something for our classes, they rarely have to. An "easy button" is always available. Very soon, some of the only authentic evidence of what students know will be the words that, in real time, come out of their mouths.

This realization can be overwhelming. Our class discussions are complex, unpredictable, and fragile. Any one thing might turn a success into a failure. Sometimes our pacing is off—we linger too long with a back-and-forth that should have been quick, or we rush students on from a fruitful exchange that deserves much more time. Every once in a while, the energy in the room is just off, our students are not as into it as we thought they should have been, or they are distracted by outside noise that we can't control. As we try to keep our most important class discussions from stalling, we are often told to look inward, examining our privileges and biases, our cultural competency. This is useful work that is important not just for many aspects of our pedagogy but also for our relationships with students.

Yet many of us have found that although such reflection has made us better *people*, it has not solved the core issue: Would-be extraordinary class discussions continue to draw blank stares. Students don't seem invested in debates that they should be fired up about. The class gets to *that* awesome part of *that* awesome book, only to respond with a collective shrug. We have done the work, finding culturally representative sources and centering our students' lived experiences, and well, *meh*. Kids might participate, but it feels dry and rote, the kind of robotic hand raising that seems more like checking off the participation-grade box (or offering favors to an increasingly desperate teacher). How can we bring more oomph to our class discussions? Infuse them with fire? Or at the very least, keep them from repeatedly falling flat?

Discussion Prompting, Put to the Test

This concern never loomed larger than it did in the spring of 2020 and, for some of us, the entirety of the next school year. March hit, and suddenly, we had to teach from our dining room tables and home offices, as our children played or went to school themselves in the next room. A beautifully decorated classroom was now a Zoom or Google Meet window. A well-planned seating arrangement was now a participants list. Most important, many of our students' faces were now wordless black boxes. I used to, only half-jokingly, refer to this stilted virtual experience as "teaching, without most of the fun parts."

This was a spartan moment in our careers. If we were brave enough to lead class discussions, we had only our deliberately positive faces, our strained voices, and the words that we typed into the chat. And these words—these prompts—had to be *good.* We could not supplement them with any front-of-the-classroom dramatics. We could not walk around the room and nudge kids who had their heads down. We could not read students' faces to see if our words had landed or if they were confused. Our typed words had to hook and challenge students. They had to be intriguing enough to maintain students' interests as a (hopefully) once-in-a-lifetime mix of pandemic and social unrest screamed for their attention. Our words had to compete with video games that could be played *in class* and TV shows that could be watched *in class,* both sometimes sharing the same screen as our lesson. This humbling pandemic experience pushed educators toward many realizations, most of which are still relevant as we teach in the post-pandemic world. None were more practical than this: Great discussions are sparked by great prompts, asked by an agile teacher, at the best time, to a group of students that has been rightly prepared to discuss them.

About This Book

Part I of this book will describe how to craft and refine these vital discussion prompts. Its first chapter will help teachers set goals for class discussions that are both ambitious and realistic. Its second will describe how to thoughtfully prepare to lead these powerful class discussions. Its third chapter will answer some of the most common questions about discussion prompts, then show, in detail, how to craft them. Finally, its fourth chapter will show how we teachers can keep our well-prompted discussions from falling flat.

Part II will be interactive. Readers will be provided excerpts from classroom texts and then be invited to plan discussion prompts around them. After giving readers space to do so, this book will share prompts that I (and some of my colleagues from other disciplines who were generous enough to be interviewed) have created for the same excerpts. I hope that these examples can spark interesting conversations between colleagues, or even like-minded teacher friends, who, like me, are just trying to get a little better at prompting deeper discussions.

Part I

Prompting for Success

1

Visualizing Deeper Discussions

What does the phrase *class discussion* mean to you? What does it look like? Sound like? *Feel* like? If you were to play a film of a perfect classroom discussion in your mind's eye, what would be its rising action, climax, falling action, and resolution? Would it be a thriller? A comedy? A lengthy, heavy period drama? Would hammy A-list actors dominate its dialogue?

As I review apprentice teachers' lesson plans, I often see the line, "Students will discuss ______." Sometimes, the bland verb "discuss" has been replaced with a seemingly richer verb like "review," "debate," or "consider." Occasionally, I see a more evocative phrase like, "students will *wrestle with*" or "students will *tackle*." The apprentice's ambition is the same, no matter their phrasing: They want to lead our students in a powerful discussion. Seeing this, I sometimes challenge them to play a film of the upcoming discussion in their mind's eye. Sometimes this is a struggle, so to spur their imaginations, I ask a few concrete questions, like "What's the first prompt you're going to ask? How will your follow-up prompts build—or hold on to—kids' interest?" Sometimes I ask apprentices to anticipate the mood of the discussion, with questions like, "What's the *vibe?* Will we be telling jokes? Are kids meant to be excited? Or should they be somber and reflective?"

Sometimes, I ask the apprentice to think through everyone's role, with questions like, "Which student do you anticipate will do most of the talking?" or "Which student might get a little emotional?" I almost always ask the basic, but exceedingly important, "Just how long is this discussion supposed to last?" Often, these questions are answered with silence, then, depending on how much time remains before class, a little bit of panic.

I know my film metaphor isn't perfect. A class discussion might have more in common with an improv show. Or a well-designed bridge. Or a meticulously crafted multi-course meal. But the lesson remains the same: It's best to visualize what success looks like *before* we launch a class discussion. (And not only what success looks like *to us*, but also to our students, their families, and our administrators.) Without this clear mental picture of success, we can find ourselves blithely accepting anything that feels like it. This acceptance can drag our class discussions far from their potential, day after day, year after year.

Popular Myths About Class Discussions

It's understandable why even the most seasoned teachers might struggle to visualize the best version of any class discussion, especially discussions meant to engage controversial topics. Unless our mentor teacher was a nerd about dialogic practice, reflection about our discussion planning was probably not their highest priority as they guided our apprentice teaching experience. And then, as we were getting our sea legs in our own classrooms, we rarely (if ever) received professional development specifically on leading discussions. And if the administrator or department chair who formally observes us has detailed well-thought-out advice about how we are facilitating discussions, we are certainly lucky!

Popular myths about classroom discussions are eager to fill this vacuum. These misleading ideas come from many sources: Some we see in tweets from edu-celebrities, while some appear as whispered advice from colleagues. Each of these myths can distort the film playing in our heads as we visualize a great class discussion.

Myth 1: Class Discussions Are Just Seasoning (Not the Main Course)

I attended one of the finest education programs in Pennsylvania. I learned a lot of useful strategies for teaching English language arts (ELA), many of which I still use faithfully decades later. However, among distinct courses in developmental psychology, effective assessment, literacy, and writing, there was not one course dedicated to leading class discussions. (I honestly can't even remember a lesson about it.) In Pennsylvania, teachers are formally tasked to make students better at "reading, writing, speaking, and listening" (Pennsylvania Department of Education, 2014). In most programs, *reading* and *writing* are given their own courses, while *speaking* and *listening* are folded into the whims of a methods course—if engaged at all.

This makes sense, of course. Both reading comprehension and effective writing are explicitly tested. A school's autonomy, even its funding, might depend on how well students answer multiple-choice or essay questions about a boring passage about a yacht or a bland drive through a desert. This alone is enough to encourage a hyper-focus on reading and writing. But there is also the perception that reading and writing skills are flat-out more important for students' lives, whereas speaking and listening are complementary, extra skills that well-rounded students should work on to get a "leg up." This hierarchy of importance, interestingly, doesn't vibe with what the Association of American Colleges and Universities discovered when they surveyed executives and hiring managers in 2018. According to an *Education Week* article about the study,

> Good oral communication skills got the #1 slot among the 15 job skills that executives and hiring managers identified as very important in new hires. Eight in 10 executives and 9 in 10 hiring managers said recent college graduates really need good speaking skills when they come looking for jobs. Oral communication ranked higher than critical thinking, ethical decision making, and working in teams. It's more important to company leaders than being able to write well, solve complex problems, or be innovative. (Gewertz, 2018)

Despite this—and a lifetime of corroborating anecdotal evidence from our own professional lives—many educators only work on speaking and listening *when we have time*. Activities that focus on speaking and listening are used to occasionally season certain lessons, making these moments a bit more interesting. But these discussion activities rarely get the same critical reflection as other allegedly more important elements of our practice. Without this purposeful reflection, it's easier to blame failed discussions on students' unpredictable interests or deficits in a teacher's personality. This leads to the second myth.

Myth 2: The Teacher's Personality Is the King of Discussion

In my first book *Not Light, but Fire* (2018), I had a good time making fun of dynamic teacher archetypes like those found in *Dead Poets Society* and *Dangerous Minds*. When leading professional development sessions, my most reliable laughs come from canned jokes at their expense: "Gee, I was gonna bully that kid, Mr. Kay, but since you gave that impassioned speech about safe spaces, I think he's my best friend now." (Laughter.) Or "I've been shy my whole life! Thank goodness you turned that chair backward, sat down, looked me right in my soul, and told me that my voice matters!" (Laughter.) I can usually work up a few laughs by comparing my 22-year-old physical theatricality to my current eagerness to teach from my seat. "Does *anyone* else need me to look over their essay? I'm about to sit down, and once I do, *you* come to *me*!" (Laughter.)

These jokes land mostly because the trope refuses to die. Teachers are continually lionized for endless energy and unreasonable sacrifice. In fact, until the hit show *Abbott Elementary*, the only stories told about us seemed to star iconoclastic but caring martyrs who single-handedly saved kids from systems out to destroy them. Oh, and they've *got* to be young and able-bodied! No veteran teacher can be faulted for a little eye roll. Still, when it comes to class discussions, this trope has done real and lasting damage. It's hard for many of us to picture a softer-voiced teacher leading a vibrant class discussion. It's hard for many of us to picture an older teacher, a teacher with a thick accent, or a teacher in a wheelchair leading a lively class discussion. But not only this. Crucially, many of us have only been shown one personality type for teachers capable of leading powerful class discussions: a theatrical empath, bristling with kinetic energy.

You'll never hear me say that teachers should hide their personalities. It's also cheap to suggest that some personality traits, like being funny, don't give some teachers an advantage when leading specific discussions. A naturally funny teacher might be able to present prompts in ways that make students laugh. A naturally performative teacher might engage in dramatic interactive read-alouds more effortlessly than most.

But these advantages don't have much to do with how class discussions are *designed*. Every one of us—regardless of our personalities—who is willing to work hard at crafting great prompts can lead great discussions. This brings the third myth to mind.

Myth 3: Student-Centered Means Giving Up the Keys to Discussion

The education world loves its absolutes. We are either project-based or test-driven. Late work is either refused outright or accepted without penalty. Our discipline programs are either zero-tolerance or virtually nonexistent. In some districts, we spend millions on curriculum, only to throw it all out two years later. There is a *right* way to teach kids reading and a *right* way to teach them math. All other approaches are foolish, unscientific, myopic, or even racist. Then, within a few years, we lurch back to the old way, and teachers are ordered to execute the shift with 100 percent fidelity.

This either/or stance shows up often when teachers visualize class discussions. Some of us have been advised to never be a "sage on a stage." We might have been scolded for *leading* discussions instead of *facilitating* them. Were we to make this shift, our pedagogy would be more *student-centered*. This last phrase is often interpreted to mean that our students drive our class discussions while we, the professionals, limit our role to encouraging kids from the passenger seat.

Our feelings about this passenger seat often vary. For one, it probably sounds like hell for folks who regularly teach through their own professional anxiety. These teachers thrive on knowing what to generally expect from every slideshow, activity, and assessment. The mere thought of walking into class, throwing the kids an issue, and *seeing what happens* is enough to make their heads explode. On the other side are teachers who thrive amid the unknown: folks who consider a cliff jump into the conversational abyss to be an intoxicating thrill. These teachers are less likely to be put off by laissez-faire definitions of student-centered. Either way, the absolutist vision of the passenger-seat teacher is a daydream in most schools. (And not just because some administrators won't accept the hands-off approach.) Experience has taught many of us that, in certain class discussions, a teacher giving up total control might make the same kids that we want to empower feel paradoxically less safe. When things go wrong, students look for an authority. And if that authority has relinquished *their* authority, the discussion can get ugly *quickly,* especially when tossing kids the keys links up with the fourth myth.

Myth 4: Debate Is Automatically the Best Way to Engage Controversial Topics

This myth is as simple as it is prevalent. Although debates can be very formal, they can also take the form of fun, casual, "stand over here if you believe *this;* stand over there if you believe *that*" discussion activities. In these moments, if students ask where to stand if they haven't made up their minds, we might answer with "In the middle." Or, if we are feeling less generous, we'll tell them that they *have* to pick a side for the good of the activity. Once everyone is settled, it's time for the kids to go at it.

Debates, when well-led, are awesome. Debates, when poorly led, can ruin a year's worth of relationship building. I am not anti-debate. But to believe that the best way for students to discuss a controversial topic is *automatically* to have them debate it—formally or otherwise—is to buy into a dangerous myth. There could be *many* reasons that students are not quite ready to debate a controversial issue. Maybe they don't yet know the topic well enough to debate it without dealing in (and maybe even spreading) toxic falsehoods. Maybe the social dynamics of the class are not yet ready for debate, and students will be using the academic exchange as a slick way to bully each other. Maybe there simply isn't enough time to do it responsibly. Few things are worse than kicking off a debate with 12 minutes left in class, then realizing that it very much needed 20 minutes because a kid said something wild, and we didn't have enough time to calm things down. This brings us to the fifth myth.

Myth 5: All Sides of an Issue Deserve Equal Consideration

I know I've got to tread lightly with this one, especially in the wake of "All Lives Matter," the famously disingenuous response to people like me asking the criminal justice system to stop killing us. I've got to be especially careful writing in the post-2021 education landscape, where, in many places, at least, there is a growing expectation that all teachers give equal space to all sides of more contentious issues.

Some defend this myth by making it about defending students' constitutional rights to speak their minds, but these arguments are reductive. Time and again, the courts have affirmed that students do not "shed their constitutional rights to freedom of speech or expression at the schoolhouse gate" (*Tinker v. Des Moines*). Few teachers disagree. We know that it's not our role to openly restrict student speech (except in a few special circumstances). But what professional choices should we make once students begin sharing some of their most controversial opinions? Should we encourage these students to speak provocatively, knowing that specific classmates are vulnerable to having their feelings hurt? Will we call on students who know something substantial about a controversial issue as often as we call on kids who are merely eager to share hot takes they've gleaned from social media?

Folks who perpetuate this "all sides matter equally" myth rarely engage quandaries like these in good faith. They say things like "Kids these days are too soft. They expect to be coddled all the time" and less openly antagonistic statements like "All opinions deserve equal respect." This latter statement has even been codified into law. One Texas statute reads, "Teachers who choose to discuss current events or widely debated and currently controversial issues of public policy or social affairs shall, to the best of their ability, strive to explore such issues from diverse and contending perspectives without giving deference to any one perspective" (Texas House Bill 3979, p. 2). In 2021, some in Ohio's House of Representatives tried to push through a bill meant to make educators "teach divisive concepts in an objective manner and without endorsement," including "the impartial discussion of controversial aspects of history" (Ohio House Bill 327, p. 20).

In a Texas science class, should classroom discussions give equal "deference" to contending perspectives about whether vaccines work? Should an Ohio history teacher lead "impartial" discussions about eugenic sterilization as if it were merely a "controversial aspect of history," even though thousands of people still live with the scars? When put into action as policy or practice during a class discussion, this "all sides" myth is absurdly inconsistent. If all sides of an issue deserved equal time, what about the trans student who disagrees with how their experience is represented in a novel? How about the Indigenous student who must collect participation points during laudatory Christopher Columbus discussions? Or how about the Black student who is pushed to cheer for Confederate iconography at the homecoming pep rally? (Or, worse, compete in the following game wearing a "rebels" uniform?) Say any of the aforementioned students were to bring up a salient point about any of these issues during a class discussion, and in doing so, they make their classmates as uncomfortable—for a moment at least—as these students have been made to feel for days, weeks, or years. Can a teacher engage this point academically without risking sanctions? In too many places, the answer is *no*. Until it is *yes*, it's only right that people of goodwill call this stance a myth.

The stances that are the most rooted in justice deserve the most consideration. The stances that have been the most rigorously considered deserve the most consideration. Most important, the stances that are true deserve the most consideration. Yes, our classrooms should never be hostile places for children to develop their understanding of an issue, but they should also be places where the truth is unabashedly the standard.

Myth 6: All Students Need to Speak for an Equal Amount of Time

Many of us would love to be doing anything but leading a class discussion when we are professionally observed. Discussions are unpredictable in ways that other pedagogical strategies are not. We pretty much know how the class will go when we are introducing a skill, but we never truly know if our administrator is about to witness a total collapse—students who are dramatically bored, off task, or arguing—when they observe a discussion. Many of us have even *nailed* the class discussion (at least in our heads), only to see a poor evaluation score with some version of "Do you think you could get more students involved in the conversation?" written on the form.

This feedback can be tough for us to swallow. We have been working with these students for months, and we know that some of them *really* like to talk, and some of them would rather eat dirt than raise their hands in a whole-class discussion. Often, we have worked tirelessly with students in the latter group: sidling up to them in the middle of class to compliment their work and hopefully build their confidence. We might have spoken to them before class, tipping them about the day's prompts and challenging them to raise their hand, just to get the feel of it. They might have even raised their hands—*yesterday*—when we weren't being observed! Also, to be frank, we appreciate the eager talkers. These students continually rescue us from awkward silences. They regularly find ways to connect our discussion points to something going on in their world. These energetically vocal kids are, frankly, the spark that our discussions depend on. Any feedback that implies that we should actively discourage them from speaking feels wrong. This implication also falsely assumes that more vocal students are automatically bad listeners. I've even heard it implied that these students are overprivileged and need to have this privilege checked!

Aren't some kids just quiet? Quiet doesn't automatically mean "not engaged." Quiet doesn't automatically mean "lacks confidence." It doesn't automatically mean "doesn't feel safe." It just means quiet. Some students don't enjoy speaking in front of large groups. They *can*. They just don't *want to* if there is another option. This feels like a human personality trait that any thoughtful and caring teacher's pedagogy should respect. We should, of course, help students to develop the communication skills that they need. But to think that this means that our goal should be 100 percent equal speaking time is not going to lead us to good places. It will convince us to set up artificial systems that punish students for not speaking enough. These systems trick us into valuing the *quantity* of raised hands over the *quality* of our students' contributions. This myth may also inadvertently lead to us giving our more vocal students the professional version of a cold shoulder, which might alienate the very enthusiastic voices that our class discussions depend on.

Looking Past the Myths to Five Axioms of Class Discussion

We should not let these popular myths distort our mental picture of a successful class discussion. Myths lead us to set unrealistic expectations. Myths get us into unnecessary trouble. Myths convince us to not be our natural selves in front of an exacting teenage audience that *hates* a teacher's phoniness. And if we are honest with ourselves, some of these myths have always given us pause. Maybe we've thought, "I know I'm supposed to sit back and listen, but… I'm the one with the degree!" or "Man, I don't know if these kids are ready to debate this. It just happened!" or "I don't really want to call on Billy right now. Love him, but he's a smart aleck. He's always looking for ways to annoy his classmates." But so many people have told teachers that these doubts are arrogant, cowardly, or problematic, so we are tempted to ignore our best instincts.

I'm going to propose a different starting point for our visualizations: five axioms that should survive the commonsense tests that the earlier myths fail. See what you think.

Axiom 1: Inquiry Is King

All great discussions have one thing in common, whether they exist in a classroom, a barber shop, a boardroom, or on a marriage counselor's couch: inquiry. All participants in a great discussion are *trying to figure something out.*

Sometimes it starts like this:

Barber: How you gonna tell me LeBron is the GOAT when MJ never lost a finals?

Client: How's he *not* the GOAT? All-time scoring champ, top 10 in all major categories, *and* rings for three different teams? He's been the best for decades!"

Sometimes it starts like this:

Designer: If we build this submersible the way you described in your email, materials will cost double the price. Is there a cheaper way that doesn't compromise safety?

Engineer: There might be... it depends on the kind of safety you are looking for. Your way gets us near OSHA's standard, but I think you need something sturdier.

It doesn't matter if a conversation is playful or contentious, frivolous or consequential, its best version involves two or more people trying to make sense of something through questioning it. Sometimes the inquiry is as explicit as it is in these examples. Often it is not. When I ask one of my daughters, "How was your day at school?" I am not just asking what they got up to. I am trying to figure out how this one day has contributed to their process of growing up. Did they learn anything about friendship? Did they wrestle with a math problem until it finally made sense to them? Did they work up the nerve to advocate for their needs with that teacher? (My eldest: "It was good." *Sigh.*)

Crucially, the end goal is not just to share information or opinions. Both information and opinions are steppingstones on the way to *big questions*. How do we determine the relative greatness of a pro basketball player? What's a reasonable tradeoff between passenger safety and a company's bottom line? This is what makes a discussion rich, both in the adult world and in our classrooms. Any discussion that exists just for students to share information or opinions has a cap on its potential. Kids who want to share will share and maybe answer some follow-up questions, and then we are in for an awkward silence. For prolonged engagement, we've always got to be trying to figure something, or some*one,* out. Which brings us to the next axiom.

Axiom 2: The Will to Strengthen Relationships Is the Only Thing

The legendary football coach Vince Lombardi famously said, "Winning isn't everything, but it's the only thing." The quote has become a popular slice of sports Americana, a concise way for many of us to celebrate our competitive natures. Lombardi was amplifying a phrase that had been common in coaching circles even then, and according to a reporter who covered him, the coach grew to "wish to hell [he] never said that" (NFL Films, 2021). This was because he'd meant to argue that the "*will* to win" was the "only thing" (Dure, 2015). Lombardi was trying to say that every time one of his teams took the field, they did so with winning in mind. They would never lower their standards or rest on the laurels of previous championships.

We all hear a lot about how important it is for teachers to build relationships in our classrooms. They are everything. There is no way that you picked up this book still thinking that building relationships is not important, so I won't bore you by stating the obvious. However, like Coach Lombardi, I want to make a clarification: Pre-existing classroom relationships are not as important as the genuine *will to strengthen them*. This isn't just semantics. If we believe that relationships are everything, then it makes sense to build them proactively (i.e., before class discussions), hoping that doing so will inoculate us against catastrophe. This early work is a good practice that any thoughtful teacher would recommend.

However, it's easy for us to assume that once we *have* built these relationships to a certain degree—the students are speaking respectfully, they are showing care—we should move on from relationship building. If we do so, we might forget to plan discussions that direct students' inquiry not just at our subject matter but at each other. And then, unfortunately, we might find the relationships in the room regressing as quickly as they had been built. To put it simply, the job isn't over after early successes. We must help students who have already grown close to each other to leave our class discussions knowing each other even *more* authentically. If we commit to doing so, the next axiom should come naturally.

Axiom 3: Joy Fuels Some of the Most Memorable Discussions

I am pretty good at teaching the structure of analytical writing. Students tend to leave my 9th and 10th grade ELA classroom better at basic grammar and mechanics than they were in September. We read rigorous books that push students to use nearly every tool in their comprehension toolkits. And you know what? When I speak to parents, I have *never* been complimented on these efforts. It's always, "He really liked that he got to write so many stories" or "I can't believe that she *liked* that book! I hated it in high school." Or my runaway favorite, "*Every* night, she wants to tell us what you all were talking about in class. I feel like I'm auditing it."

I was always honored by this, but I didn't *get it* until I was a parent. When my daughter went to school for the first time, all of a sudden, I found myself feeling genuinely touched when she would come home excited to tell us a story about something cool she'd discussed in class. Both my wife and I are career educators who intimately know the importance of a strong foundation, and yet, the most important thing to us is that she *likes* learning. We want her formal schooling to encourage—and not stamp out—her natural curiosity. At the most basic level, she *has* to be at school. For seven hours. It should not feel like confinement. Whether it was Ms. Alexis and Mr. Will in preschool; Lisa and Mary Beth in preK; Katie, Rachel, and Sarah in kindergarten; or Bernadette and Brian in both 1st and 2nd grades, we appreciated the moments that they made our young child—who was just beginning her school journey—laugh, smile, and dream. We love them because they prioritized joy.

We don't talk about fun enough in secondary education, and it's a shame. For example, the "I can't believe she *likes* that book" remark from some parents makes me so sad. It also always seems to be the classics, which I teach sparingly, that spark this kind of comment. But those old books can be so spicy! *The Odyssey*? Battles, intrigue, and sex! *Lord of the Flies?* A bunch of kids lose their natural minds! We shout "Whoa!" and gasp when Bigger Thomas kills Mary Dalton in *Native Son*. Discussions are a way to show students that something is funny, scary, or exciting when otherwise they might not see it.

Frankly, these revelations keep teachers necessary in this AI era of schooling. In our discussions, kids share a laugh or a gasp that makes them feel like fellow *human* travelers to a cool, fun place. If joy is there to be had, we've got to grab it as systemically as we can, which is helped by the next axiom.

Axiom 4: Routines Matter

Nationally, around 12.5 percent of a fitness club's new members sign up during the first weeks of the calendar year (Bats, 2022; Connor, 2019; de Bruin 2021). However, a large percentage of these new folks cancel their memberships soon after, 50 percent before the end of January, and as high as 80 percent within the first five months (Bats, 2022; Connor, 2019; de Bruin, 2021). Any gym that does not find ways to manage this problem will fail. Knowing this, clubs have spent a lot of energy figuring out how to hold on to as many "New Year, New Me" members as possible. It begins with acknowledging that people who join during the January rush are often just setting off on their personal fitness journeys. They walk into a gym not knowing how to use equipment or perform certain exercises. Some start trying exercises at random, copying what they've seen and hoping for the best. After a month or so of this approach, they grow discouraged and fall off. Knowing this, fitness clubs constantly try to flatten the learning curve by showing new folks specific routines. The Planet Fitness chain commits wholly to this, dedicating a large section of each of their gyms to a scripted 30-minute workout. This area has 20 numbered stations, and each has a placard with specific exercise instructions. This, along with all manner of support through phone apps, is meant to give people the comfort and confidence of a *routine* as early as possible. Then, hopefully, they will stay around.

In many ways, this is the story of teachers' relationship with class discussions. We are inspired to make our pedagogy more dialogic, but we are unsure how to do so. So, we test cool-sounding discussion strategies that we've seen on TV or heard about at a conference. We try these strategies more or less randomly. After a month or so of this approach, we (or our students) sometimes get frustrated at uneven results.

Our class discussions must settle into a routine. Ideally, this routine should include a few whole-class activities (like interactive read-alouds), a few small-group activities (like fishbowls and Socratic seminars), and a few one-on-one activities (like peer reviews or interviews). None of these discussion activities are inherently better than others, but some are better for certain students, in certain moments. (More on this in Chapter 2.) We get to be the professionals who decide which activities make our Planet Fitness-esque circuit. But once we do, we've got to commit to the workout, at least for a while. Our students deserve the chance *to get good* at a discussion activity through repetition and reflection. And so do we! This is especially important with activities that provide chances for joy. I think back on specific discussion activities, such as interviewing characters from books, that my students loved but that I only did once a year when that specific chapter in that specific book rolled around. It seems such a waste to not make that joyful activity something kids can look forward to trying again soon.

Axiom 5: And Yet, Surprises Also Matter!

Many of us have a few signature classroom catchphrases. My students often imitate my ominous announcement of a quiz ("Let's go. Blank sheet of paper, name, date, stream!") or my jaunty reminder to keep their writing minds open ("Don't marry that idea—date it for a while!"). Later in the year, I'm known to playfully tease students, reminding them that "I am *so* boring. I am *so* predictable." If it's Monday, we *are* starting the class by sharing our good news. If it's Friday, the class *will* start with silent sustained reading. All recorded small-group discussions must be seven minutes or longer. If we are discussing a reading as a whole class, we *will* read it aloud, just like we did yesterday and the day before. (And yes, if I assigned that reading, I'm *quizzing* that reading. I love seeing students chuckle at my "Ain't no 'pop' quizzes in this class! You knew about this, so save all that sighing for someone else.")

And yet, within these routines, it helps to find space for surprises. Especially with class discussions. It's one thing to commit to regular interactive read-alouds. It's another to have *all* of these interactive read-alouds feature the teacher performing as the star protagonist. It's one thing to host small-group discussions twice a week. It's another to make them always about the core texts and never about supplementary sources or the real world. It's one thing to rely on daily turn-and-talks. It's another to have *all* turn-and-talks end with sharing with the whole class.

Furthermore, our routines don't remove the need for the occasional splash discussion activity. We might not typically gamify our debates by adding points, but maybe keeping score might make a specific exchange more fun. Maybe a whole-class discussion could benefit from inverting the power dynamic, with the teacher sitting among the students while a kid offers the prompts. Guest appearances in discussions are often fun; sometimes an expert or an author stops by, and sometimes it's just a colleague from another discipline. Maybe the discussion venue shifts outside because the weather is just so darn lovely. These moments aren't the everyday meat and potatoes. They are the dessert: not offered after every meal but on the menu regardless just in case the sweet tooth calls.

Keeping It Real

Realism gets a bad rap in many educational spaces. It is too often taken as a signal of low expectations and dismissed as an aversion to rigor. To be a realist is to be pessimistic. We are told to prefer the aspirational, the inspirational, the paradigm-shifting. However, realism has not lost its luster in most classrooms. Most teachers want to cut through the noise and find out what *works*. Not what *would work* if only our school had more money or different students. Not what *would work* if our administrations or communities were more supportive. Not what *would work* if we had more time. Dreaming is a luxury that many of us do not have.

This is why I have chosen to start this book by examining how we picture a successful class discussion. It is a waste of both our time and our energy trying to live up to goals that ultimately make no sense. We frustrate ourselves and annoy our students when we allow myths to frame what it means to do a good job. On the other hand, a realistic picture leads to realistic goals. Working toward realistic goals feels worthwhile, even when we fall short of them. Realistic goals—helped by the axioms in this chapter—are easy to communicate to students, families, and administrators. Far from signaling low expectations or an absence of rigor, realistic goals show that a teacher is committing to the hard work of figuring out how to meet their students where they are and then planning discussions that thoughtfully move them forward.

If someone were to ask me what a roaring success would look like—the high but unabashedly realistic standard that I hold myself to—my mind would draw the following pictures.

In Whole-Class Discussions

1. Most of the students are tracking the current speaker with their eyes. Those who are not are looking down at their notebooks.
2. Classroom discussion procedures, like taking notes on what classmates are saying, are performed with an easy rhythm of expectation. I have to remind students but not *too much*.
3. Although the enthusiastically verbal students are doing most of the talking, there is a reliable sprinkling of other volunteers.
4. Most students are not just speaking to me but to each other. This includes asking each other authentic questions.
5. At least a few students are smiling at one point or another. Some even laugh (good-naturedly, of course) at either something in the text or at a joke that I or their classmates make.

In One-on-One or Small-Group Discussions

1. As I walk around, most students are engaged in the prompt that I've asked them to discuss.
2. The students are not just taking turns answering the prompt—they are asking each other follow-up questions.
3. When students return to whole-class formats of discussions, they can cite something that their classmate said during the more intimate one-on-one or small-group discussions.

4. Similarly, when asked to produce an artifact of learning (essay, project, etc.), students can cite something that a classmate said during one-on-one or small-group discussions.

This unapologetic realism doesn't just provide a healthy standard for our own class discussions. It also gives like-minded teachers (and administrators) a productive framework for both examining and supporting discussions that we observe in other teachers' classrooms. I often sit down with colleagues or apprentice teachers after class discussions that they thought had gone poorly. When I ask why these teachers seem down, they talk about the three students who had put their heads on their desks. Or about how only a few students did most of the volunteering. Or about how small groups took too long to stop talking. These frustrations are valid, of course. But sometimes, in the same class, I saw multiple students taking notes on the discussion. A few vocal students had spoken more often than others, but at least a few other kids had raised hands to answer the more interesting prompts. It might have been annoying to get the small groups to transition back into a whole-class format, but I had been walking around, and some of the most disruptive students were still talking because they were *still interested!*

If unrealistic, myth-driven goals are not deliberately counterbalanced with reasonable goals, a teacher can be tempted to overcorrect. We can throw out essentially good stuff instead of merely tweaking it. We can decide that students can't be trusted to discuss issues in small groups. We can create systems that artificially push students to raise their hands when they have nothing to say. In the name of balancing all sides of an issue, we can put students in socially awkward situations that they'll have to deal with in the lunchroom and playground, long after they are out of our sight. Frustration might even cause us to forget that some students who'd put their heads down had sports practice that morning and that the right discussion isn't about disengagement—it's about going to bed earlier and remembering to eat breakfast. In these moments, a colleague, a mentor, a department chair, or an administrator might be needed to recalibrate our expectations. At times, we *all* need a reminder that grabbing and maintaining the attention of 20–35 unique humans is *hard.* Leading kids in a thoughtful discussion is even more difficult. There is nothing wrong with steady, incremental progress toward reasonable goals. We should remind each other of that as often as possible. Once we have a reasonable and clear picture in our heads, we can start the next chapter's work of preparing a great class discussion.

2

Preparing to Prompt Deeper Discussions

Some educators specialize in turning boring texts into powerful class discussions. They always seem to find the most interesting questions to ask, and they make the process look *so easy*, like a gifted outfielder tracking down and catching a deep fly ball.

As you can probably tell from the last chapter, I have never trusted this "natural" teacher archetype. Educators do not magically pull great questions from thin air. Great questions are the byproduct of *a lot* of hidden work, much of which happens early in the planning process. Sure, for some, this process might be aided by an extroverted personality. But for every social butterfly, there are teachers like me who wouldn't call themselves natural conversationalists. Regardless of where we are on this spectrum, *all* of us stand to benefit from being more conscious of, and conscientious about, the work that helps us prepare great questions.

How to *Reread* for a Class Discussion

Many of the best class discussions start days, months, or even years before we even meet the students who will participate in them. These discussions are born not only in professional spaces like our classrooms and home offices but also in unexpected spaces and times—during trips with a spouse to the movies or moments on the couch with the kids watching Netflix. These discussions are sparked the moment we engage a text and think, "This could work."

This text could be a *primary text* that anchors our official curriculum or a *supplementary text* that seasons it (more on this later). Either way, we must first *re*read, *re*watch, or *re*listen to this text, focusing on its specific role as fuel for discourse. This is not a small shift. Here are a few major differences between our first encounter with a text and when we *re*engage it to prepare a class discussion.

When We Read for Ourselves, We Are Often Trusting

When we spend our own money on *Time* or *National Geographic* subscriptions, we do so expecting real stories. In our heavily fragmented news media landscape, we have the luxury of tuning into whichever channel offers whatever truth that we support so that when a journalist speaks, we can take their words as gospel. When we read a memoir, we choose to believe in the author's ability to recall specific dialogue from quite a long time ago. We assume that most novelists have designed reliable narrators until they prove otherwise beyond a reasonable doubt.

This trust is understandable when we consider research on psychology. In his bestselling book *Talking to Strangers,* Malcolm Gladwell (2019) describes psychologist Tim Levine's *truth default theory,* which argues that "our operating assumption is that the people that we are dealing with are honest" (p. 73). The book cites several interesting experiments from Levine and others to argue, "We do not behave, in other words, like sober-minded scientists, slowly gathering evidence of the truth or falsity of something before reaching a conclusion. We do the opposite. We start by believing. And we *stop* believing only when our doubts and misgivings rise to the point where we can no longer explain them away" (Gladwell, 2019, p. 74). Although many people, myself included, might bristle at this notion, it settles in nicely when we consider the cynical alternative: never trusting a reporter, food inspector, or banking system. It's downright peaceful to sit down with a book and fundamentally *trust* the stories held within.

When We Reread for a Class Discussion, We Should Be Skeptical

Although a reader's stubborn trust is natural, it builds a shaky foundation for high-quality class discussions. Frankly, as teachers reread any text to begin preparing a discussion, skepticism must enter the chat. We should suddenly be open to the possibility that an author has different or more complex motivations than she openly states. Or that he might not know as much about the topic as he claims to know. Or that events happened differently than the author described them. Every text should immediately become an artifact that represents *one author's perspective*. Had someone else written it, many takeaways might be very different. This same skepticism applies when we zoom in on specific fictional characters. Sure, the bard *says* that Odysseus weeps on Calypso's island because he misses Penelope. But does he? I seem to remember an unnecessary side trip on the way home from Troy where the so-called hero says he "sacked the city, killed the men, but as for the wives and plunder, that rich haul we dragged away from the place" (Homer, 1996, p. 212). Was he *really* in such a rush?

Frankly, any text's merest hint of hero worship should make our Spidey senses tingle. Hero worship makes for boring class discussions, especially with teenagers who have complex relationships with authority. The moment teens detect that a teacher's goal is merely to *appreciate* William Shakespeare, Harper Lee, or the Founding Fathers, most of their brains go on autopilot. Conversely, the more a teacher rolls with teens' instinct to question authority, the more likely they will be to meaningfully invest in the conversation.

But it is more than keeping kids interested. The most basic definitions of discourse involve communication, which in turn means "an exchange of ideas and information." If there is only one acceptable idea, there isn't much else to exchange. Ideas flow from the top down: a teacher asking questions to confirm an author's brilliance or an icon's singular heroism. When that one-way spigot closes, the conversation runs dry.

When We Read for Ourselves, We Make Connections to Our Own Lives

I love historical fiction, as it combines my two favorite passions, history and storytelling. And if that historical fiction can be about sports, like John Grisham's *Calico Joe*? As a varsity coach and unapologetic sports fan, I am in! If that historical fiction can be about the Civil War, like Michael Shaara's *The Killer Angels*? As the son of a Civil War buff whose favorite movie is 1993's *Gettysburg*, I am in! If that historical fiction can have some time travel, like Stephen King's *11.22.63?* As a teacher who spent many years teaching Octavia Butler's *Kindred* (a genre-bending blend of primary slave narrative and time travel), I am *so* in. Similarly, whenever a story takes place in the 20th century, I notice how close events are to 1914 (my grandmother's birth year), 1947 (my dad's), and 1983 (mine). I think, "I wonder what Grandma was doing then?" or "I bet my dad watched that on the news!" or "I was born the next month!" The connection to my lived experience is the cherry atop my favorite genre.

Multiple theories explain both our eagerness to make personal connections and the efficacy of doing so. Reader response theory, for instance, argues that all reading is a transactional process, where readers bring unique backgrounds and experiences to every text (Rosenblatt, 1994). These experiences allow us to have our own special moment with each book, each one affecting us differently than any other reader. In addition to this, schema theory suggests that readers actively construct meaning by integrating new information with existing knowledge, which has always been influenced by life experiences (Piaget, 1954). The more we connect our lives to a text, the better we understand it.

When We *Reread* for a Class Discussion, We Should Search for Connections to Our Students' Lives

Many things get much easier as our first year of teaching recedes in the rearview mirror. Now that we have an idea of how long activities are going to take, we find ourselves being more efficient with our lesson planning. Now that we've seen all sorts of student behavior, we are calmer in the face of classroom management issues. We may have even learned how to say no when asked to take on too many extraneous tasks. I, for one, will always remember the shift in thinking the second I held my newborn daughter in my arms. From then on, I was just a little slower to call my students my "kids." It was so much easier to keep school concerns *at school* when I had my own little human to raise.

One thing, however, gets progressively harder with every passing year: knowing how to connect texts to our students' lives. When we were young—especially those of us who teach at the secondary level—we listened to the same music as our students. We were on the same social media platforms. We watched similar movies and streamed the same shows. Then, astonishingly, we became 28, 36, and 52, while every new batch of freshmen stubbornly continued to meet us at 14. At the beginning of our careers, it took much less effort to connect a text we were reading to a popular song, bestselling video game, or explosive social media trend that our students would recognize. But if we are not regularly listening to students' music, playing their video games, or scrolling through the same social media apps, those connections take *research*. We must have at least a passing idea of what is popular globally and locally, even if we get this information from our students themselves via informal conversations and student interest surveys.

Thankfully, it's not just about rereading texts to notice connections to popular culture. It is more important that we reread to notice connections to more universal aspects of young people's lives. I have already mentioned that teenagers are universally wrestling with the concept of authority. They are also developing their understanding of which risks are reasonable. They are trying to determine what healthy romantic and platonic relationships look like. They are afraid of what sort of irreparable damage the generations before them have done to their neighborhoods, the country, and the planet. Although it may be an uphill climb to connect texts to the most viral trends, it is much simpler to look for anything in a text that connects to what it has *always* felt like to be a kid.

When We Read for Ourselves, Learning the Content Is the Goal

I love when I have enough time to grab a highlighter and mark off parts of a book that I want to remember. I rarely have a strong idea about how I will ever *use* the lines that I am marking, but I collect them all the same. I didn't go to school for psychology or economics, but when I highlighted Daniel Kahneman's *Thinking Fast and Slow,* I felt like both a psychologist and an economist. I didn't go to school for sports science, but when I highlighted David Epstein's *The Sports Gene,* I felt like a top-notch physical trainer. I did not study the law, but marking up Melvin I. Urofsky's *Dissent and the Supreme Court* made me feel like an esteemed Supreme Court justice. And it's not just nonfiction. I took the highlighter to Flynn Berry's *Northern Spy* so that I could better understand Ireland's sectarian conflict, and I gave the same treatment to Julia Alvarez's *In the Time of Butterflies* to better understand Trujillo's dictatorship in the Dominican Republic. There are few things in a reader's life more satisfying than a dog-eared page splashed with neon ink, riddled with both underlined words and scribbled notes in the margins. (In fact, there is no greater compliment to an author than someone bringing them a book to be signed that shows physical signs of being well-loved.)

The interesting stuff found in books and other texts makes us feel smarter. It both kicks off and strengthens relationships by giving us something to contribute to conversations. It makes us better parents, spouses, and colleagues. Regularly reading and interacting with interesting stuff makes our brains healthier, possibly even staving off Alzheimer's disease, as a group of nuns famously found out in 2001 (Belluck, 2001). There are so many benefits to reading a text for the sole purpose of learning its content.

When We *Reread* for a Class Discussion, a Text's Larger Themes Are Often More Important Than Its Content

Some of our most consistently powerful discussions often center the themes that a text tackles, not the content that it covers. Yes, this content may be interesting to learn, especially for students who entered the class excited to engage it. But discussions that *only* consist of questions like "What happened?" or "What was this about?" or "What did we learn?" have a natural limit: Once these questions have been answered, the conversation has no natural place to go. On the other hand, when we ask students to explore a text's larger *themes*, our discussions have a chance to push into greater territory. The best of these discussions taps into centuries-old conversations about loyalty and betrayal, beauty and ugliness, life and death, and so on—rich issues that people have been passionately discussing for centuries.

Focusing on themes also makes it much easier for us to thread seemingly disparate conversations over the course of the year. In doing so, we can sequentially develop students' understanding of an issue. In this book, I continually reference three books from my current 10th grade curriculum: *Lord of the Flies, The Book Thief,* and *Native Son.* In these books, three different authors write about three different protagonists living in three different settings; yet if I decide to center the theme of *justice* in all three books, I can use multiple class discussions to guide my students toward a thorough, multilayered understanding of the topic.

When We Read for Ourselves, Our Personal Enjoyment Is Often the Goal

When I was a little boy, my dad would read me the Mark Twain books that he'd loved as a kid, *The Adventures of Tom Sawyer* and *Huckleberry Finn.* He also knew that as a semi-rambunctious kid, I might identify with the smart-mouthed protagonists. My grandmother, knowing that I liked animals and (at that time!) fervently wanted to be a farmer, would read me James Herriot's wholesome classics, *All Creatures Great and Small* and *All Things Bright and Beautiful.* As I got older, my mom and I had our own personal book club, where we took a liking to Robert Morgan's books, like *Gap Creek.* She knew that I still had an interest in naturalistic settings that were different than my urban Philly neighborhood. Growing up, the adults in my life were fast to show me that everything I could possibly enjoy could be found in a good book. I'll always appreciate that.

This foundation taught me that I deserve to like any book that I am reading. Even as I learn about heavy topics, I deserve to find *something* about the writing entertaining. Perhaps an author seasons the tragedy with a quick wit, like Trevor Noah's treatment of apartheid in *Born a Crime*. Perhaps they interview odd people that I would otherwise dismiss, like Will Sommer does with QAnon adherents in *Trust the Plan*. Perhaps they use a good love story and a healthy dose of adventure to teach me about brutal history and otherwise-boring architecture, like Ken Follett does in my all-time favorite book, *The Pillars of the Earth*. I shouldn't need to learn tough stuff the way that some folks take a stiff drink. I, and all readers, deserve fruity flavors, a few pretty colors, and a nice glass.

Similarly, this foundation taught me that I deserve to read so-called fluff. The kind of books that stand to teach me absolutely nothing. Spy novels. Romance novels. Horror stories. Superhero comic books. It's OK to read a book simply because it will make me laugh, gasp, or, if I need a good cry, *cry*. I don't need to justify my reading preferences to anyone, and neither does anyone else.

When We *Reread* for a Class Discussion, Sparking Student Joy Is Often the Goal

Few things sadden me more than the sharp decline in children who read for fun. According to a 2020 survey conducted by the National Assessment of Educational Progress, the share of American 9- to 13-year-olds who read for fun on their own time almost daily is at the lowest levels since the 1980s. Even more concerning, among 13-year-olds, 28 percent of Asian students said they read for fun almost every day, along with 20 percent of White students (Schaeffer, 2021). These shares are larger than the shares of Black (15 percent) and Hispanic (10 percent) students who said the same (Schaeffer, 2021). There are many theories that try to explain these phenomena (too many screens, over-standardized and boring reading instruction, and a lack of representation in books). Still, the chief takeaway is the same: Many students have an increasingly joyless relationship with reading anything longer than a tweet, meme, or caption.

It is convenient to blame teachers for this state of affairs, just like we are blamed for every other ill that plagues society. I, for one, reject the notion that our profession is completely at fault. This problem is not *just* ours to solve. Still, we must admit that our decisions influence students' personal reading habits, and these decisions begin the first time we read a text with the goal of planning a discussion. When doing so, our eyes must highlight parts of the text that will not just stir up students' awe and passion but, if possible, make them *laugh*. It is understandable that we might focus only on the writing skills that an author is modeling, or that we might think of a text merely as a vehicle to practice tested skills like defining an author's purpose, making inferences, or comprehending cause and effect. These goals are important, and in many places are how we are held accountable for doing our jobs. But to focus solely on the sections of a text that model good writing or present a smooth way to practice a tested standard is to miss an opportunity to use our influence to link reading with fun.

I referenced *The Odyssey* earlier in this chapter. Having taught it to freshmen for over a decade, I both know it well and am surprised at how often folks are surprised that 14-year-olds can enjoy it. When first reading it to plan conversations, I was hyper-aware that if I didn't fixate on making it *fun*, young students would fixate on how *hard* it was. So each planning session became a mining expedition for both gasps and giggles. Yes, we would need to discuss the story's in medias res opening and complex sequencing. This would help kids score a few points higher on Pennsylvania's high-stakes Keystone Test. But I would also need to poke a little fun at Calypso's super-thirsty fixation with the hero. I would also need to have a good time with Circe turning Odysseus's men into pigs, failing to do so with Odysseus, and then trying to seduce him to get out of her bind. We might even need to act out the part where, in the same chapter, one of these men gets super drunk and falls off the roof.

Not every student would find these sections funny, exciting, or dramatic. But crucially, every student would see their teacher making an honest effort to make them so. I'm OK with being known for *trying* to make a book fun, even if I fail almost as often as I succeed. Often, the effort alone leads to enough of a good time. (Me: "C'mon, *nothing*?"

Students, giggling: "Sorry, Mr. Kay.") And in a class of 33 students, I'm willing to bet that at least 10 enjoyed the moment, which is 10 more than if I hadn't at least tried to model enjoying the text.

Hunting for Supplements

Once we have reread a text with the aforementioned fresh eyes, we might be tempted to jump directly into writing discussion prompts. However, there are a few more crucial steps, the next of which is very much connected to my suggestion to consider classroom texts thematically: actively hunting for supplementary materials.

We teachers are often fully aware of how a certain text or idea applies to the greater world. With all our education and lived experience, the connections are glaringly obvious. Many students, however, do not automatically see the same connections—which means that they default to putting every text in its own silo. This isolation might spoil the upcoming class discussion in multiple ways. Here are a few:

- Students who are naturally "just not that into" a particular text don't see a reason to engage, if the discussion is *just* going to be about that text.
- Students might not see how their personal lives relate to a text if they are not nudged to do so by a supplement.
- Students might not see why a text is ultimately worth discussing, if they don't see how it has affected the greater world.
- Students might not naturally use the text as a mentor text for their own work, unless they discuss how others have done so.
- Students might not recognize the significance of a text's positionality, without making comparisons to supplemental texts from different cultural backgrounds.

For these reasons (and more), the hunt for supplements should not be treated as extra work. It is a crucial step, one that is often what pushes a text from boring to exciting and a class discussion from good to *great*. Let's explore how supplementary sources can liven up discussions about a text that many students initially consider dry—the aforementioned *Lord of the Flies*. This book has multiple story beats that are ripe for discussion—especially if we have reread it with any of the last section's lenses:

1. The boys crash on the island.
2. They realize that they are stranded.
3. They try to set up a temporary society.
4. Some of them have problems with the leadership.
5. Many of them stop following the rules.
6. The "rightful" leader realizes that he doesn't have as much power as he feels like he should.
7. A group of dissenters splits off into a separate society.
8. "Smaller" acts of violence build up the boys' tolerance for bloodshed.
9. A more significant act of violence changes *everything.*
10. The "more" civilized boys beg everyone to not lose their humanity before it's too late.
11. A rescue and, possibly, a reckoning.

Lord of the Flies is fiction. But every one of its story beats has a parallel in David Grann's (2023) nonfiction *The Wager: A Tale of Shipwreck, Mutiny, and Murder.* In it, the crew of a British warship is shipwrecked on a desolate island in Patagonia in 1742. The men have a harrowing experience that not only hits all the above beats, but also introduces a culture clash with the Kawésqar, an Indigenous people from the area. (The Kawésqar try to help, showing the starving British sailors how to gather food, but the British end up trying to abuse the Kawésqar women and steal their canoes. This convinces the Indigenous folks that saving the Europeans isn't worth the trouble, and they abandon them in the middle of the night.) Even as they are starving, the crew from the Wager never lose their sense of ethnic and racial superiority, a sentiment that is also reflected in *Lord of the Flies,* when Piggy screams, "Which is better—to be a pack of painted Indians like you are, or to be sensible like Ralph is?" (Golding, 1954, p. 180).

This beat-for-beat similarity can deepen the conversations that any teacher has about *Lord of the Flies.* Of course, students don't have to read *The Wager* in full. But we can pull one- to three-page excerpts from sections that we know kids will find interesting. As climactic moments come up in the primary text, we can show them how real people dealt with the same issue. Then we can ask the simple yet powerful prompts that make supplementary texts so useful:

- "How is [moment from primary text] similar to [moment from supplementary text]?"
- "How is [moment from primary text] different from [moment from supplementary text]?"
- "Why might [specific similarities or differences] be important?"
- "What does [moment from supplementary text] teach us about [moment from primary text]?"
- "How does [moment from supplementary text] influence how we feel about [moment from primary text]?"

Of course, a supplementary text does not have to match the primary text beat for beat to have a powerful impact. During the *Lord of the Flies* unit, one of my favorite resources is a *Guardian* piece titled "The Real Lord of the Flies: What Happened When Six Boys Were Shipwrecked for 15 Months." Unlike the sailors from the Wager, the real Tongan boys in this story did *not* descend into savagery. In fact, "the boys had set up a small commune with food garden, hollowed-out tree trunks to store rainwater, a gymnasium with curious weights, a badminton court, [and] chicken pens... all from handiwork, an old knife blade and much determination" (Bregman, 2020). While the characters in *Lord of the Flies* never had the discipline to maintain the signal fire meant to attract attention from passing ships, the Tongans tended a flame for over a year. While the fictional boys in Golding's famous allegory skirted necessary work (as did the sailors on the Wager), the Tongans "agreed to work in teams of two, drawing up a strict roster for garden, kitchen and guard duty" (Bregman, 2020). And most important, while the boys on the fictional island killed Simon, Piggy, and (by neglect) countless "littleuns," and the men on the Wager not only committed direct murder but also stranded attempted thieves on rocky inlets to die, "Sometimes [the Tongan boys] quarreled, but whenever that happened they solved it by imposing a time-out" (Bregman, 2020). Shorter supplementary sources like this *Guardian* piece can use versions of the same basic prompts—and require a little less work from a teacher to prepare.

Supplementary texts also give us a chance to include multimedia resources, which is especially crucial for students who have a more, let's say, adversarial relationship with reading. Before discovering both *The Wager* and the *Guardian* article, I was fond of using videos of the Milgram Experiment to link the allegorical world of the *Lord of the Flies* to the reality of human cruelty. (Some of my favorite Milgram prompts are in Part II of this book.) Throughout *Lord of the Flies,* a teacher could also show students allegorical movies, so that students can discuss symbolism with lower stakes. I often start the unit with a Claymation video that tells Plato's famous cave allegory (Bullhead Entertainment, 2008). (This discussion is detailed in the next chapter.) Then either we watch a full allegorical movie as a class, or I give them a choice of allegorical cartoons to analyze in groups. When I decide to watch a movie with the entire class, we often watch *Pleasantville,* because I know that, in addition to being a cool allegory, the book burning scene will set us up nicely for *The Book Thief* conversations later in the year. When I choose to give students small-group choices, it's usually *Avatar, Turning Red, The Lego Movie, Spirited Away,* and *Zootopia.* Most students tend to find at least one of their passions represented in the choices, from fighting racism and imperialism to making sense of one's developing identity and coming to peace with it.

Small-group discussions about these more choice-driven supplements are sparked with prompts like this: "The allegory in [insert your group's movie title] used symbolism to make a commentary on ______. Ultimately, the symbols were effective [or not effective] at this goal. Why or why not?" Meanwhile, when looking at *Pleasantville* as a whole class, I've used prompts like this: "The allegory of *Pleasantville* has two central female characters, Jennifer and Betty. Each of these women go through a symbolic shift that, for the '90s, seems profound. But do these characters unintentionally communicate damaging messages to the film's 1998 audience?" and "The attempted assaults on 'Colored' citizens in *Pleasantville* seem to be the first incidents of violence in the town. However, could a reasonable person argue that the 'pleasant' black-and-white '50s era sitcom town from the beginning of the film is more violent than it is during the unrest?" I could, of course, craft similar prompts about *The Matrix, Big Fish,* or any allegorical film the kids might appreciate as a supplement to the main *Lord of the Flies* allegory.

As mentioned earlier, supplementary texts, whether they are engaged continually (like *The Wager*) or dabbled in once or twice (like the *Guardian* article or the practice allegories), give teachers the chance to help students see how multiple cultures and experiences relate to the main text. I often lead teachers in professional development about classroom race discussions. In a popular session, I describe how we might surface and discuss race issues in texts that aren't normally discussed. I tend to use the *Lord of the Flies* "pack of painted Indians" line from earlier in this section as an example. A teacher wrote me a lovely email after one of the sessions, saying, "My whiteness and Euro-centric education sometimes leaves me in the 'developing' column of the 'noticing racial inequities rubric' in old, dead, white men books. I'm pretty competent from the gender lens as that is my lived experience, but I'm still learning to deepen my view in noticing issues of race where they aren't surface level—like they are in *Lord of the Flies.*" Excited as always to engage teachers who reach out, I wrote back, asking what she was teaching. She replied, "*Macbeth.*"

I, of course, had nothing. At least nothing that had anything to do with race. I'd taught and discussed *Macbeth* with 9th graders for years. Most of the conversations had rightfully been about ambition, tyranny, and fate. Lady Macbeth's monologues and conversations with her husband can prompt awesome discussions about gender roles. But no race discussions. *Macbeth* can be a tough book for my Philly-area students to see themselves in, especially my students of color. This email inspired me to peek back through my old Macbeth unit to see how I had handled this, and with relief, I found an answer. Back in the day, I'd compared the violently ambitious Macbeth to Bumpy Johnson and Frank Lucus in scenes from two of my favorite movies, 1997's *Hoodlum* and 2007's *American Gangster.* (Cersei Lannister from *Game of Thrones* and Claire Underwood from *House of Cards* also provided great TV scenes to work with, though neither helped much with racial representation.) I gleefully replied to the email, saying, "We can also compare *Macbeth* to similar stories from different cultures. For instance, what are other stories, from different cultures and starring people of color, that engage the theme of unbridled ambition? Same with tyranny, regicide, etc. Are there any differences between what Shakespeare's audience in England expected vs. what is expected in thematically similar stories from other cultures?"

With thoughtful supplements, our students can see how people from various races and cultures fit into any primary text's thematic conversations. This does not, of course, replace our responsibility to teach primary texts that provide "mirrors, windows, and sliding glass doors" (Bishop, 1990) to various cultures—including kids' own. This inclusion will always be important. But in a diverse curriculum, no culture is *always* centered. Among all their benefits, thoughtful supplements ensure that students from traditionally marginalized identities can see and discuss themselves even in moments where their stories do not have a curriculum's center stage.

Picking the Best Discussion Format

After rereading the text with fresh eyes and hunting for supplementary sources, we should think about which format might work best with an upcoming class discussion. This is often an unconscious decision—we might default to the formats that were our favorite back when we were a student or the ones that our students (or observing administrators) have praised. Many of us have, over the years, expanded our discussion facilitation toolkit to include more than a few activities. In my first book, *Not Light, but Fire* (2018), I used the term "conversational package" to describe the bucket "of structural [discussion] variations that fit our personal vision and our students' situations" (p. 75). I went on to argue that all dialogic teachers should try to get comfortable with a couple of whole-class discussion strategies (like debates), a couple of small-group discussion activities (like Socratic seminars), and a couple of one-on-one discussion activities (like interviews).

Each bucket of activities has both advantages and limitations. Whole-class activities give the teacher the most control. They also tend to—for better or worse—put students on stage. Small-group activities allow more students to talk in a given amount of time. They also—for better or worse—remove the teacher from immediate earshot. One-on-one activities remove all spectators except the person being spoken to. They also—for better or worse—give students nowhere to hide from awkward silences. None of the three buckets hold inherently flawless discussion activities. But certain activities might be better for certain discussions, with certain kids.

When to Choose Whole-Class Formats

As just mentioned, whole-class activities theoretically give teachers a great degree of control over the discussion. We often lead these activities from the front of the classroom, all eyes, supposedly, on us. (Yes, many of us do ask students to look at whomever is talking. But then, *back to us*!) We ask the prompts. We call on the participants. With our eyes on the clock, we cut short certain exchanges or even end the entire discussion. We encourage more of what we want to hear and discourage what we don't. If someone talks out of line or says something inappropriate, we are in a position to both notice and react swiftly to it. This degree of control might be a little out of fashion nowadays, but, as I mentioned in the first chapter of this book, it's a myth that students need the keys to *everything*. Sometimes the teacher needs to drive. Especially when the destination is teaching students how to both speak and listen to each other as scholars.

This control might be one of the most important factors when deciding if a whole-class activity fits a certain discussion. This decision is complex, with answers that are often counterintuitive. For instance, one might think that more sensitive discussions—those requiring a good deal of vulnerability—shouldn't be held with the whole class watching. Still, experience has taught me that the number of spectators may not be as important as whether students feel like their teacher can deftly direct the prompting and, if necessary, shut down unsafe behavior.

For example, I teach Patricia McCormick's (2006) *SOLD* to high school freshmen. The book uses a poetic style to tell the story of a young girl from Nepal who is kidnapped and trafficked into sex slavery.

SOLD is a heavy story, but an important one, inspired by McCormick's interviews with women and girls who have been trafficked. (Ever conscious of my privilege as a man, and the uneven power dynamic in the classroom between teachers and students, I am often torn about including this book in my curriculum. Yet, year after year, students of all genders—and races—tell me that they appreciated learning about slavery that does not center the antebellum South.) McCormick is judicious with her depictions of both rape and sexual assault. So much so that she only includes one scene where Lakshmi, the main character, is raped. I give students the option to skip this reading, assuring them that it won't be quizzed. We do, however, discuss McCormick's decision to limit direct descriptions of rape. This authorial restraint is *only* discussed in whole-class formats, for a few reasons. First, I want to make sure that, terminology-wise, students understand—from me, the classroom authority—that Lakshmi *is* being raped. It's disappointing how quickly students begin to use phrases like "have sex with" and "get with" to describe what is going on in the book. Kids use these phrases even more in small-group and one-on-one formats. This benign language diminishes the importance of the book and creates space for victim blaming.

The second reason for limiting this conversation to whole-class formats is related: I want to have ironclad control over this specific discussion. We are going to discuss McCormick's authorial restraint, *and nothing else.* The content is too sensitive for too many students for their classmates to feel like they can speak haphazardly or debate each other aggressively. There are many times when I want students to feel free to ask each other pointed follow-up questions. This is not one of those times.

With these thoughts (and others) in mind, it might be best to choose a whole-class format if the following situations apply:

- The discussion requires a distinct framing.
- The discussion might drift to an unsafe place if not for a teacher's control.
- The discussion relies on a teacher's specific expertise.
- The prompting needs to happen in a specific order for the discourse to make sense to students.

- The students need to, for whatever reason, hear the teacher's voice *often* to stay productive.

When to Choose Small-Group Formats

With small-group discussions, teachers begin to cede some of this control. Beyond a teacher's initial prompt, it's up to students to keep a conversation not just going but *productive*. Both this autonomy and this responsibility are tricky. Think back to the maelstrom that was the 2020–21 school year. After moving our classes online, many of us remember being excited about the prospect of splitting students into breakout rooms for discussions, only to find out that many of our students *hated* these breakout rooms. There was way too much pressure. Nobody wanted to be the kid who took the discussion "too seriously" in the teacher's absence. (This was like being the kid who reminded the teacher to give homework!) Of course, the accountability piece is easier in a physical classroom, but still, the difficulty never really goes away. However, when students *are* invested (as hopefully they will be if asked the sort of powerful prompts discussed in the next chapter), the responsibility to keep the discussion going can be empowering, if not thrilling. The discussion is *their baby*. It's only still alive because students have chosen to *feed* it.

For an example of a discussion that works well in small groups, let's return to *SOLD*. When discussing McCormick's book, my students must learn about and discuss the various pernicious systems that sustain human trafficking. To make our discussions just about individual human cruelty would be to miss a big opportunity. Students should learn how these systems are developed and maintained. They should discuss how, with enough political and personal will, these systems can also be destroyed. I have found the famous Stanford Prison Experiment to be a fine supplement for *SOLD*. (Yes, I make sure that students know the experiment's gaping flaws.) In part of the BBC documentary that I show students, Professor Phillip Zimbardo describes what he calls a "degradation process" (Im, 2017). He does not directly define the term, and I don't define it for my students. Instead, I ask them to guess what they think the term means, using what they are noticing in the documentary. Seeing the "guards" delousing the "prisoners," calling them foul names, and making them clean toilets with their bare hands, my students conclude that the term probably means the act of systemically breaking someone down. I ask them, in small groups, to list other situations where they see deliberate degradation processes. Students' answers vary, from "prisons" and "basic training" to (unfortunately) some classrooms. Then, in these groups, I ask students to point out any parts of the brothel's brutality in *SOLD* that seem like cogs in a deliberate degradation process (as opposed to examples of individualized, random cruelty). Then, the small groups share with the larger class. Choosing a small-group structure means that not only do more students get to talk, but each group gets to feel ownership over its unique analysis of the issue.

With these thoughts (and others) in mind, it might be best to choose a small-group format if the following situations apply:

- Students would benefit from a little less direct supervision from a teacher.
- Students would benefit from the freedom to ask their own follow-up prompts.
- Students would enjoy the challenge of figuring out or solving a specific issue as a team.
- Students would benefit from certain specific groupings (i.e., kids from different cultures and different genders) in a specific discussion.
- There are friend groups and academic relationships that a teacher would like to encourage through a specific discussion.

When to Choose One-on-One Formats

One-on-one discussion activities are the most private option. There are no spectators. Unless a teacher happens to be standing directly above the exchange, students can trust that their voices won't be overheard above the din. Because of this, they might feel more comfortable revealing stuff that might otherwise get them fussed at ("I didn't do the reading. Did you?"). They can ask each other awkward or embarrassing questions ("This is too hard. Do you get what he is talking about?"). Students have the power to *completely* shrug off the question and discuss something else—or surreptitiously scroll through their phones. Nobody would be the wiser.

This lack of spectators does have advantages. Whole-class activities can be performative and occasionally stir up unfortunate "look at me!" behaviors, like trolling and grandstanding. There's little incentive to show off when you only have an audience of one. Some of the quieter kids mentioned in the last chapter thrive when asked to speak with only one classmate. And finally, there is the simple math: Pairing students gives them the most time to speak. After speaking in a whole-class discussion, a student might not speak again for 30 minutes. It's a little better with a small group. But in a one-on-one conversation, students get the chance to follow up on what they've said, clarify their reasoning, and answer questions more patiently. Again, *if* they are invested in the prompt.

Let's return, for the last time, to *SOLD*. Early in the book, after Lakshmi gets her period, her mother takes her aside to teach her how to be a woman. Among other advice, she says,

> Now, you must carry yourself with modesty, bow your head in the presence of men, and cover yourself with your shawl.
> Never look a man in the eye.
> Never allow yourself to be alone with a man who is not family. (McCormick, 2006, p. 15)

As I reread *SOLD* to prepare for class discussions, this section immediately brought Jamaica Kinkaid's award-winning short story *Girl* to mind as a supplement. In it, an Antiguan mother advises her daughter, who seems to be around Lakshmi's age. Among other things, she says, "You mustn't speak to wharf-rat boys, not even to give directions" and "this is the way that you behave in the presence of men who don't know you very well. And this way they won't recognize immediately the slut I have warned you against becoming" (Kinkaid, 1978). As I reread, I was intrigued that two stories from vastly different cultures had such strikingly similar mother-to-daughter preparing-for-womanhood-in-a-misogynistic-society moments. Many questions emerged: What do students make of the moms' rough language? Is it tough love, abuse, or something in between? Are these sorts of conversations dated? Have students received similar advice from adults in their lives? How are these conversations different with boys? How many students, regardless of gender, have had "how to be a woman/man" conversations? Why do parents have them? Have these conversations been effective, destructive, or something in between? The list went on and on. I discovered that the best structure for these questions was one-on-one, mostly because of the extended opportunity for students to tease out and justify their thinking. I also figured, seemingly correctly, that this was a time when the lack of spectators *did* make students more willing to share personal stories. Even so, I preemptively told students that they didn't *have to* reveal any connections to their lives if they didn't want to. They could even vaguely talk about another teen's experience. They could also count on not being rushed.

With these thoughts (and others) in mind, it might be best to choose a one-on-one format if the following situations apply:

- Students, for whatever reason, would benefit from the complete absence of spectators.
- Students would enjoy the chance to discuss an idea with the least amount of time pressure.
- Students are being asked to look back at a source multiple times over the course of a discussion.
- Students are helping each other to workshop something (like a peer review).
- We are asking a specific series of prompts to help students build closer academic or personal relationships.

Ultimately, choosing a structure for an upcoming class discussion still depends on our tastes and preferences. We like some activities more than others, and that's fine. Similarly, our students will find some activities fun and others tedious. And they will disagree about which activities fit into which category. This, again, is fine.

It's just important that we don't make the decision all about which activities we—or a group of our students—*like*. After rereading the text and finding powerful supplements, let's make sure that we have the specific advantages and disadvantages of each structure in mind as we pick which one we're going to try.

Winning Early

Many of the truisms about coaching youth sports apply neatly to leading students in meaningful class discussions. We know, for instance, that a coach's preparation is key. We put our teams in the best position to win when we study game film from our opponents' previous games. This provides the information needed to plan useful practices and craft a strong game plan. The critical eye we need, as we look at game film, is much like the critical eye we bring to rereading a text. Similarly, coaches need to ask themselves what an upcoming opponent has in common with those that our team has already played. This helps them to familiarize athletes with upcoming challenges by associating them with challenges that they have already faced (and possibly overcome). Athletes will then, hopefully, go into the upcoming game with confidence. This confidence is precisely why a teacher should search for supplementary materials that make the core text more accessible or more interesting. Finally, coaches must make a game plan determining which system of plays or strategies will help their athletes overcome a specific obstacle. A teacher must use this same deliberate thoughtfulness when selecting from the hundreds of possible discussion structures and activities.

The early work described in this chapter is so often the elusive element that—in its absence—has kept our conversations from consistently thriving. We make a discussion plan based on our more personal reading of a text. Or we miss an opportunity to make a text relevant to more students by connecting it to something more familiar. Or we choose the "wrong" structure for what is otherwise the "right" discussion. If you take nothing else from this chapter, please walk away understanding the importance of slowing down and thoughtfully preparing for the moment. When we do so, the prompts that we'll design in the next chapter have the best chance of scoring *big*.

3

Crafting Great Prompts

After we have visualized a class discussion's success, reread its core text thoughtfully, sought out the perfect supplements, and picked structures that we think will work, it's *finally* time to craft our discussion prompts. Each of Merriam-Webster's definitions for the transitive verb "to prompt" has exciting ramifications for teachers. The first is "to move to action," while another is "to serve as the inciting cause of" (Merriam-Webster, n.d.). In a sense, discussion prompts are like the thousands of controlled explosions occurring every minute inside a car's engine: They must be incendiary (at least at some level) to propel us along, yet without a teacher's control, these blasts become unsafe. Another Merriam-Webster definition of "to prompt" is "to assist (one acting or reciting) by suggesting or saying the next words of something forgotten or imperfectly learned" (n.d.). The latter part of this definition ("something forgotten or imperfectly learned") sounds *exactly* like where most students are after engaging with a text by themselves. Even if they have earnestly done the reading and taken good notes, their understanding is further solidified by asking and answering questions about it. Students who have *not* read a text as patiently or actively (or even at all) find themselves even more served by engaging questions about it thoughtfully.

For the purposes of this book, I'll loosely define the noun "prompt" as "a question that inspires students to interact thoughtfully with a text."

The Importance of Priming

In their bestselling book about reading across the curriculum, *Subjects Matter,* Harvey Daniels and Steven Zemelman (2004) asked readers to make sense of a *very* strange passage. Before I move on, feel free to try to make sense of it yourself:

> With hocked gems financing him, our hero bravely defied all scornful laughter that tried to prevent his scheme. "Your eyes deceived," he had said. "An egg not a table correctly typifies this unexplored entity." Now three sturdy sisters sought proof. Forging along, sometimes through calm vastness, yet more often over turbulent peaks and valleys, days became weeks as many doubters spread fearful rumors about the edge. At last from somewhere, welcomed winged creatures appeared, signifying momentous success. (p. 25)

This, of course, is gibberish. More specifically, it is a word puzzle that Daniels and Zemelman use to demonstrate the importance of prior knowledge as we try to understand something new. On their own, phrases like "an egg not a table" and "sturdy sisters" mean nothing. But if we are given a solitary clue—in this case, the word "Columbus"—all of a sudden, the passage makes sense. It is now clear that "an egg not a table" references Columbus's thought that the world was flat. Similarly, we now know the "three sturdy sisters" as the Nina, the Pinta, and the Santa Maria. The authors explain that the word "Columbus" served as a key that unlocked "a dozen terms that, a minute earlier, were deeply mysterious" (2004, p. 26). A short explanation of schema theory follows. Basically, cognitive researchers have found that we store knowledge in mental patterns called *schemata,* which store and connect all the information in our minds related to a topic. So the word "Columbus" brought "words, pictures, stories, maps, images, readings, attitudes, and feelings" to our consciousness (2004, p. 26). Daniels and Zemelman wrote that, ultimately, "all the information you needed to read the passage was right in your head, but until the right schema was activated, you 'couldn't read' the passage" (2004, p. 26).

Often, our first job when crafting prompts is activating whatever schemas will be necessary for the ensuing discussion. These *priming prompts* stir up and center relevant memories, from both inside and outside kids' formal schooling. For example, when introducing characterization, I have asked students, "If your friend called you from a strange number and their voice was distorted, how would you know it's them *without* them introducing themselves?" This is often followed up with "Let's say that your friend's social media was hacked, and the imposter reached out to you. How would you know that it wasn't your friend?" As these questions are discussed—and often laughed about—students remember the distinct speech and writing habits that make their friends unique. With this information at the top of their minds, they can more easily understand the *next* point: that fictional characters should be made to speak, write, and act in unique ways as well.

Priming prompts can also, as illustrated in the Columbus example, help students get unstuck once a discussion has already started. Let's say students in a gym class are discussing the rules and strategies of hockey before splitting into teams and playing for the first time. In many areas in the country, students are not likely to know much about hockey. When discussing strategy for the first time, students might get hung up on why it might be important that a team deliberately keep some defenders back when they are attacking. But a savvy teacher could ask, "How many of you played soccer as a tiny kid, like under 6 years old? How about basketball? Do you remember how all the little kids used to run down the field or the court, all in a bunch?" Students might giggle at this memory. The teacher could then ask, "What did the coaches yell out?" The students would say something like "Spread out!" or "Give them space!" The teacher could then ask a simple "Why?" Students would remember learning (often the hard way) that it is easier in both sports to dribble without being crowded. Others would remember that it is also easier to pass to a teammate who is farther away because that teammate's defender is also farther away. Still, other students would remember youth coaches yelling at them to "Get back!" when the other team had the ball and then realizing that it was easier to do so in both sports if they weren't all running around in a pile. It is the same, then, in an unfamiliar sport like hockey.

Finally, priming prompts are meant to get kids excited for the upcoming discussion. There are many ways to do this, but perhaps the most consistently successful tactic is directly connecting the discussion to students' out-of-school lives—a strategy helped by the specific rereading habits described in the last chapter. For example, only a few weeks before writing this section, my sophomore class was discussing domestic surveillance, specifically Edward Snowden and the National Security Agency. This topic is, on its surface, fascinating, but it can lead to a surprisingly boring class discussion if students are not primed thoughtfully. In the first of back-to-back class periods, I told students about the fear that many Americans in my generation felt after 9/11, admitting that many of us were willing to give up some civil liberties to feel protected from terrorism. The kids paid attention, but the ensuing conversation lacked the spice that I'd expected. When the next group of students came in, I simply asked, "So how many of you have a cover for your webcam?" Puzzled, nobody raised their hands. I followed their intrigued silence with, "So if your laptop camera could actually be turned on, without your permission or knowledge, at *any* point of the day or night, . . . and people in the government could watch you, . . . how would you feel about that?" *Boom.* Every eye was on me. A forest of hands was in the air. From here, we followed the same discussion thread as the first class, but my students were *much* more invested.

I ended the last chapter by showing the stark similarities between preparing athletes for a sporting contest and preparing ourselves (and students) for a great class discussion. That applies here, too. Just about every scoring strategy in the sports world requires some sort of priming. Volleyball players set a ball before it can be spiked. Boxers stick a few jabs before throwing the big haymaker. Basketball players freeze an opponent with a few size-up moves before blowing past them to the hoop. The list goes on, and every example echoes a teacher asking the question that perfectly sets students up for heavier prompts to follow.

Moving from Priming Prompts to Core Prompts

The next step is designing *core prompts*—the questions that inspire the most important exchanges between students. Here are a couple of the more common questions that pop to mind when we think of core class discussion prompts.

How Long Should a Core Prompt Be?

During discussion planning, our prompts might be lengthy, but by the time these questions get to students, the sweet spot is one to three sentences. The more information that students must keep in their working memory, the harder it will be for them to reserve the bandwidth needed to engage the prompt thoughtfully.

Let's say that it is the beginning of the school year, and a class of freshmen have read Sandra Cisneros's (1991) wonderful short story "Eleven." The story describes a particularly bad moment that a student named Rachel has on her 11th birthday. One of her classmates finds a gross, stinky sweater in their classroom and tells the teacher that she thinks it belongs to Rachel. Though Rachel says it isn't hers, the teacher makes her claim it. When Rachel nudges it to the tip of her desk, the teacher forces her to wear it. The abhorrent cottage cheese smell and the embarrassment are enough to make Rachel burst into tears. Moments later, another student claims the sweater. The teacher, crucially, does not apologize for failing to listen. Or for bullying the child into putting on a repulsive sweater in front of everyone.

Consider the following prompt: "How do you think this incident made Rachel feel? Why? Have you ever felt like this? If Rachel was currently a 14-year-old freshman at [insert your school], sitting right next to you, how might this experience have affected her identity? Her relationship with current classmates and teachers? Her willingness to learn?" This prompt, which sounds a lot like what I hear from conscientious apprentice teachers every September, is full of thoughtful questions, all of which are related. Yet it also asks kids to keep *a lot* in their heads at one time.

Now consider this shortened version: "If Rachel was currently a 14-year-old freshman at [insert your school], how might this experience have affected her identity? Her relationships with current classmates and teachers?" Notice how we have cut both the first question about Rachel's feelings and the second one that connects the text to students' lives. This may seem to contradict my earlier advice to connect to students' experiences, but this edit actually does the opposite. This character analysis and the personal connection each deserve *their own* prompt. We do not want *some* of our students answering the intensely personal, "Have you ever felt like this?" while *other* students are busy tackling a weighty theoretical question about an aged-up Rachel. When prompts are kept short, students get to focus on one thing at a time. They can also more easily pay attention to and respectfully build off each other's contributions because everyone is responding to the same thing.

Lastly, notice how my edited prompt *still* provides a little bit of help text. The added "Her relationship with current classmates and teachers?" gives kids more ways to access the main question (about the aged-up Rachel's identity). Here, I anticipate that students might not fully understand the question, so it makes sense to nudge kids toward possible ways to tackle it. But notice how I've still edited out the "Her willingness to learn?" bit. This language was cut for a different, and more flexible, reason: It felt like *too much* help text for my students, like I was leading a witness. What if they wanted to say something else about Rachel's relationships with teachers? Of course, you might make a different call. We all get to decide how much help text, if any, to tag onto the beginning or end of our discussion prompts—a decision mostly informed by our relationships with students and our understanding of what they need.

How Hard Should a Core Prompt Be?

There are two ways to interpret this common question. The first measures the raw difficulty of a prompt's language, and the second measures the level of rigorous thought needed to answer it. The first is uncomplicated and will be discussed here. The second is complex and will be addressed in the next section. Put simply, we should favor accessibility over elevated, erudite, jargon-y language. Just like we don't want students exhausting their limited working memories processing too many questions, we also don't want them spending forever figuring out *what was just asked.*

This doesn't mean that we can't use a prompt's language to grow our students' scholarly vocabulary. It just means that we must be mindful about how we do it. Imagine a discussion about Richard Wright's (1944) *Black Boy.* The early part of his bestselling memoir describes how his family was affected by his father's abandonment. Young Wright then found himself not only facing crippling hunger but also having to take over new responsibilities that would have been his father's. In a famous passage, he was beaten up and robbed by a group of boys on the way to the store to get food. Ignoring his tears, his mother gave him more money and a stick; she told him that he would not be allowed back into the house unless he completed his chore, defending himself violently if necessary. Wright did, eventually beating the boys with the stick and even challenging their parents to come outside and get some, too.

Now consider the following discussion prompt: "Do you think that Richard Wright's mom did the right thing? Why or why not? How does your answer relate to cultural relativism?" This prompt starts with an easy-to-understand dichotomy and plain language. (Was it "the right thing" to do?) It might be useful to openly acknowledge that students' answers might be more complex than a simple yes or no. It might also be helpful to define what we mean by "right" (beneficial, harmful, moral, toxic, etc.). Again, we always get to decide how much help text to provide, but there is a clear benefit to presenting the first part of this prompt simply. We are saving students' limited bandwidth for a tougher task: connecting their answers to their (in this case, previously taught) understanding of cultural relativism.

If we want students to consider the consequences of using one culture's standards to judge another culture's parenting customs, we've got to clear the deck of *other* challenging vocabulary and concepts. Think about it. We are not only asking students to remember a previously taught definition of cultural relativism. We are also asking them to remember previously taught definitions of culture that include race, family, neighborhood, socioeconomic status, and more. Should there be a different parenting code for different families, in different neighborhoods, at different times in U.S. history? Were they, as children, taught to turn the other cheek, or did Mom say, "Don't start fights, but you better finish them!"? As students form thoughtful answers about the most important part of the prompt, *all* of these thoughts are percolating in students' heads. This takes a lot of energy. Therefore, we need to keep the less important language as simple as possible.

The Anatomy of a Great Core Prompt

With the two most common questions out of the way, let's dig deeper into the core of what makes a core discussion prompt great. How can carefully chosen words spark a spirited, lengthy, academically rigorous conversation?

Grant Wiggins and Jay McTighe provide a useful framework in their seminal book, *Understanding by Design* (2005). In it, they argue that there are six "facets of understanding." In an ASCD whitepaper about the topic, they suggest that these facets could thoughtfully be used to "develop, select, or critique assessment tasks and prompts" (McTighe & Wiggins, 2014, p. 8). The facets are not meant to be hierarchical, nor is every prompt meant to satisfy all six of them. They are merely tools that we use to clarify our intent and sharpen the language that we use in our prompts. Here are the six facets, each with an illustrative classroom example of how to use it to design better core discussion prompts.

Facet 1: Explanation

Students can explain concepts, principles, and processes by putting them in their own words, teaching them to others, justifying their answers, and showing their reasoning.

If there is one phrase for teachers to remember when writing core discussion prompts, it's "Show your work." It is much more important that our students thoughtfully articulate and defend (and, if need be, *adjust*) their reasoning than it is that they state the "right" answer. This means that, as a rule, binary questions (those that can be answered with a yes or no, right or wrong, good or bad, effective or ineffective) rarely become the foundation of good discussions without some sort of "Why?" tagged onto the prompt. Class discussions generally take off because students agree, disagree, or wish to complicate some element of each other's *reasoning,* and our prompts should regularly require them to do so.

Consider the following discussion about Markus Zusak's *The Book Thief.*

The Book Thief is set in Nazi Germany. The protagonist, Liesel Meminger, is the daughter of communist parents who were taken—and presumably killed—by the Nazis in the beginning of the book. She was sent to live with a foster family in a fictional German town named Molching. The plot centers Liesel's developing relationship with both her foster family and the Jewish man that they start hiding in their basement. In the latter third of the book, Zusak introduces a motif of people being forcibly marched through the streets of Molching on the way to concentration camps. In the first march scene, Liesel's foster father Hans offers bread to an older Jewish man who is stumbling with hunger and is immediately whipped by SS men. A few pages later, there is another forced march, and Liesel and her friend drop bread on the street for the Jews to pick up. By the time of the third forced march, the Jewish man that they've been hiding has been caught, and Liesel finds him among the captives. She runs to him, and in an emotional scene, both are discovered and whipped by the SS.

When discussing this section of *The Book Thief,* a teacher might prime the discussion by asking students if they remember what a motif is. (If the term has not been taught, this part of the book could certainly be used to introduce it.) A teacher might continue by asking students why an author would choose to either introduce or return to a motif. If we don't want our priming to be as direct, we might ask students if they recognize which narrative technique the author has used in this part of the text. We would do this, hoping that a volunteer raises her hand to say, "It's a motif!" This popular priming technique can be useful in places—getting it right gives kids something to be proud of—but it also comes with risks. Many of us have tried this only to be met with an awkward silence that kills the discussion's vibe before it has a chance to establish itself. Also, asking students, "What technique is this?" is more open-ended than it may seem. We might see "Motif!" as the obvious answer. But it's easy to imagine a student answering, "Descriptive language!" or "Tension!" or "Character development!" and they would not be wrong. A teacher would then have to choose between shifting the main discussion to match these responses or gently saying a version of "You're right! But that's not what I'm looking for." Of course, most students can handle this rejection without a hitch. But we still risk discouragement from our more sensitive kids.

After priming the discussion by reviewing the concept of motifs, a teacher could start asking core prompts that encourage students to justify answers and show reasoning. Such prompting might start with "What are the similarities and differences between the three forced march scenes?" The students could sketch out Venn diagrams in their notebooks before sharing. From here, the teacher could ask, "What point do you think Zusak is trying to make with these similarities and differences?" We could even tag a little bit of help text to the prompt, pointing students toward a specific theme with something like, "What points might Zusak be making about *bravery*? Especially in the face of overwhelming force?" I've had plenty of success asking kids, "Is what Hans doing *brave* or is it kinda... *selfish*?" Considering that he is actively hiding both a Jewish person in his basement *and* Liesel (who would be in danger if the Nazis found out that she was the child of communists) in plain sight, one could argue that his kindness to a stranger is drawing attention to his family at the worst possible time.

Help text or not, it is crucial that we challenge students to explain and justify whatever assertions they make. In my class, a debate about Zusak's point often follows—as kids wrestle over the idea that a brave act can *also* be selfish or, in a common student phrasing, "stupid." When trying to suss out Zusak's possible reason for the motif, some students look back at their Venn diagrams and compare Hans's bravery to Liesel's, noting the difference between the actions of a principled adult and those made by an impressionable child. Others take a more expansive view, noting that *The Book Thief* is a work of young adult literature, which often has the same moralistic messages that children's books have, only communicated via more mature subject matter. These kids combine this observation with prior knowledge from various anti-bullying campaigns, arguing that the author is using the motif to highlight the difference between a bystander (who witnesses bullying and does nothing) and an upstander (who stands up for the oppressed).

Facet 2: Perspective

Students can both see the big picture and recognize different points of view.

We are all in a classroom together for a reason, whether the room is physical or virtual. Teachers, students, special guests, visiting authors, field trip tour guides, and chaperoning parents are all together—at the same time—so that they might hopefully share and understand (even if they don't agree with) different perspectives on an issue. Often, these perspectives vary according to age and experience. Teachers, for instance, are not only older than our students, but we also usually attended college to teach whatever we are teaching. Our students, however, know more about their home cultures than we do, and older kids often know *much* more about popular culture than we do, try as we might to keep up. Students and teachers of color often see certain issues differently than White members of the school community, but not in a monolithic sense. We all have many identities, some of them marginalized, some privileged, all influencing our perspective on the content and skills being taught, learned, and discussed. It follows, then, that students don't fully understand an issue until they can recognize and articulate the various perspectives that different people—or characters—might bring to it.

Consider discussions about two texts that have already been mentioned in this book.

First, the aforementioned section of *The Book Thief.* When discussing the forced march motif, it can be tempting to isolate the perspectives of Liesel, Hans, and the rest of the German main characters. Good discussions can be had there. However, without a teacher's intervention, students will rarely discuss the perspective of the Jewish characters in the scene. This is understandable (especially in the first two forced march scenes) because Max is the only named Jewish main character, and he isn't there yet. Still, students don't really *get* the scenes if they don't discuss Hans's and Liesel's actions from the perspective of a Jewish person being forced to march to a concentration camp.

The core prompt is often deceptively simple. Something like, "What do you think the old man in the scene is thinking when Hans gives him the bread?" The answer is somewhat obvious, as the author wrote that the man "fell to his knees and held Papa's shins. He buried his face between them and thanked him" (Zusak, 2005, p. 394). When students point this out, I've then asked them *why* he was so thankful. Again, they point to the author's line on the next page that says, "If nothing else, the old man would die like a human. Or at least with the thought that he was" (p. 395). Then, crucially, I ask students to think about the *other* Jewish people in the crowd, the ones "watching this small, futile miracle" (p. 394). I ask, "What do you think might be going through their minds as they see this display? And why?" This sort of prompt tends to work well as a quick turn-and-talk, maybe 30 seconds or so. Just long enough to share an opinion and listen to another.

The responses to this prompt are often lively. Some brave students think back to times when they were bullied and share how much they wished someone would have stepped in, even if it were only symbolic. Others say Hans seemed to make the old man's already horrible situation worse. Hans *had* gotten him whipped. These kids point out the distinct possibility that Hans's intervention could have so angered the SS men that they might whip prisoners who had the misfortune of being nearby. Other students question if the act mattered at all to most of the Jewish people in the street, because, after looking at the scene, they "streamed by like human water" (Zusak, 2005, p. 394). Why was it written this way? Were the people so focused on their own situations to care deeply about a solitary non-Jewish man doing his good deed? These prompts can certainly be paired with supplementary sources like the graphic novel *Maus* that describe these sorts of death marches from a Jewish perspective.

For another example of this facet in action, consider a discussion about Sandra Cisneros's (1991) short story "Eleven," mentioned earlier in this chapter. You'll remember that young Rachel is forced to wear a dirty sweater that is not hers. She then cries uncontrollably and is embarrassed. But right near the end of the story, Rachel says, "That stupid Phyllis Lopez, who is even dumber than Sylvia Saldívar, says she remembers the red sweater is hers!" (p. 9). Rachel then sullenly takes it off, grumpy that her teacher "pretends like everything's okay" (p. 9). When students discuss this scene, it is understandable that they focus on mean Mrs. Price and crying Rachel. They are the protagonist and villain of the story. However, there is also the matter of Phyllis Lopez and what it must have been like to witness this entire exchange about her soiled sweater. There are more than a few prompts to make kids engage her perspective. A teacher could directly ask, "What do you think was going through Phyllis's mind as she watched this scene?" Or maybe, "Why do you think Phyllis remained silent until the bell rang for lunch?" Or "What do you make of Rachel calling Phyllis 'stupid'? What can we learn about either these girls' relationship or Phyllis's social standing in the class?" It begins to dawn on students that Phyllis might be poor, and even if she isn't, she is still probably a rung or two lower than our protagonist on the 6th grade social ladder. This perspective, when discussed, adds a fascinating layer to the story. Does stepping in to help someone who calls her stupid—even if it leads to teasing—make Phyllis the real hero of the story? A few students even wonder if the sweater isn't hers at all, and she is just stepping in to relieve Rachel of her embarrassment. Others wonder if Sandra Cisneros is using Phyllis to force careful readers to wrestle with the choices that poverty forces on folks: Either Phyllis claims the embarrassing sweater, or she trudges into the schoolyard cold without one.

Facet 3: Empathy

Students can display empathy by perceiving sensitively and "walking in someone else's shoes."

This facet of understanding strongly depends on the previous one. If students cannot recognize and articulate the various perspectives present in an issue, they will not be able to empathize with these perspectives. McTighe and Wiggins define "empathy" as "perceiving sensitively" (2014, p. 5). There is a progression, then, between a student seeing multiple sides of an issue and *caring* about what they see. A teacher's thoughtful prompts can aid in this progression.

Let's consider a social studies class discussion about the Constitution and Supreme Court case law. My sophomores tend to enjoy this unit, mostly because there are multiple landmark cases to discuss that directly involve their passions, rights, and futures. Multiple sources can be found online (e.g., Jacobs, 2007) that list various versions of "Supreme Court Cases Every Kid Should Know" that highlight cases like *Tinker v. Des Moines* (concerning the right to express yourself at school), *New Jersey v. T.L.O.* (concerning privacy rights at school), and *Ingraham v. Wright* (concerning the right of schools to use corporal punishment). A teacher can then move from any of these attention-grabbers to Supreme Court cases that either gave people rights or took them away with a specific interpretation of the Constitution. These could include not just older, famous cases like *Plessy v. Ferguson* (which allowed Jim Crow segregation) and *Brown v. Board of Education* (which made Jim Crow segregation unconstitutional), but newer ones like *Obergefell v. Hodges* (which struck down state laws limiting marriage to one man and one woman) and *Dobbs v. Jackson* (which, in overturning *Roe v. Wade*, allowed states to ban abortion).

These discussions are, by their very nature, sensitive. Students' initial opinions are likely to be informed by both their lived experiences and their relative exposure to the result of the case. (By exposure, I mean whether they can see their lives being directly affected by the ruling. Black students, for instance, are more likely to feel exposed to the *Brown* decision. Girls are likely to feel more exposed to the *Dobbs* decision. LGBTQ+ students are more likely to feel more exposed to the *Obergefell* decision.) This exposure might understandably lead to heightened vulnerability. It might also lead to heightened passion when responding to prompts. Our most basic responsibility, then, is to make sure that kids are taken care of throughout these discussions. This means, among other things, that both we and their classmates are listening patiently to them. We must also make sure that we both acknowledge and respect that what is academic or political to others might be visceral to them.

This responsibility does come with an opportunity. If we prompt discussions about issues like Supreme Court case law well, we can help students develop an understanding of how other people's experiences, hopes, and dreams inform how they look at our legal system. We might even get them to care about what they see.

For instance, let's say that students have read the opinions in *Dobbs v. Jackson* and *Obergefell v. Hodges.* Because the language can be dense, I tend to pull five important quotes from both the opinion and any available dissents. Both sets of quotes go on a slideshow that students read and discuss. Students then type answers to the following prompts into an online discussion forum: "How might folks in the impacted community find their day-to-day lives to be different immediately after these rulings? The way they think about themselves? The way they think about their futures?" Students type responses to at least two classmates before we discuss as a whole class. This slow pace is deliberate because kids need time to process both their answers and responses.

This language—and especially the help text tagged onto the main prompt—asks students to put themselves into the shoes of people who feel exposed to the possible aftermath of both rulings. In the *Obergefell* case, students must engage with Justice Kennedy's assertion in the majority opinion:

> Same-sex couples are consigned to an instability many opposite-sex couples would deem intolerable in their own lives. As the State itself makes marriage all the more precious by the significance it attaches to it, exclusion from that status has the effect of teaching that gays and lesbians are unequal in important respects. It demeans gays and lesbians for the State to lock them out of a central institution of the Nation's society. (p. 17)

In the *Dobbs* case, they must engage this idea in the dissent from Justices Breyer, Kagan, and Sotomayor:

> As of today, this Court holds, a State can always force a woman to give birth, prohibiting even the earliest abortions. . . . Some women, especially women of means, will find ways around the State's assertion of power. Others—those without money or childcare or the ability to take time off from work—will not be so fortunate. Maybe they will try an unsafe

> method of abortion, and come to physical harm, or even die. Maybe they will undergo pregnancy and have a child, but at significant personal or familial cost. At the least, they will incur the cost of losing control of their lives. The Constitution will, today's majority holds, provide no shield, despite its guarantees of liberty and equality for all. (p. 4)

In using these prompts to respond to these texts, students must—regardless of their own sex, sexual orientation, political leanings, and lived experiences—put themselves into other people's shoes for at least a few minutes. (In Part II of this book, you will see a class discussion about safe injection sites that my colleague leads in his health class. There, too, you'll see prompts meant to get kids to humbly acknowledge—and hopefully care about—what someone else might be feeling.) From this empathetic position, students can tackle a more complex prompt like "Many people anticipate that the majority's reasoning in *Dobbs* will endanger the ruling in *Obergefell*. Both the court's opinion and Sotomayor's dissent mention this idea directly. Do you agree or disagree that the logic of one ruling will eventually threaten the other? Why or why not?" Again, students start by genuinely acknowledging that certain communities feel threatened by the *Dobbs* ruling and where the ruling might lead. From this baseline empathy, however, students are encouraged to critically engage the justices' *logic*. This is different from just asking kids their general opinions on abortion or marriage equality. We are instead asking them to wrestle with the central argument in the *Dobbs* majority opinion delivered by Justice Alito:

> The Constitution makes no reference to abortion, and no such right is implicitly protected by any constitutional provision, including the one on which the defenders of *Roe* and *Casey* now chiefly rely—the Due Process Clause of the Fourteenth Amendment. That provision has been held to guarantee some rights that are not mentioned in the Constitution, but any such right must be "deeply rooted in this Nation's history and tradition" and "implicit in the concept of ordered liberty." (p. 5)

Exchanges between students may be passionate, but a carefully worded prompt makes the discussion less likely to lose its academic validity amid the heat.

Facet 4: Interpretation

Students can make sense of data, text, and experience through images, analogies, stories, and models.

As seen with the last facet, sometimes class discussions involve an idea that is flat-out *hard* for kids to fully wrap their heads around. When this happens, many students face the temptation to quit trying to make sense of the idea, choosing instead to quietly (or destructively) wait the tough discussion out. As we try our best to discourage this habit, we must realize that the thoughtful wording and deliberate sequencing of our prompts can encourage kids to chew on a complex idea until it's digestible.

Let's consider one of the more developmentally difficult concepts to regularly appear in secondary school conversations: allegorical symbolism. We ask students to read, watch, or listen to a story that *means* something bigger than what it literally *says*. This is like showing students one of those autostereogram images that were popular when I was a kid, the ones that look like a bunch of random tightly packed dots until we deliberately cross our eyes and *boom!* A 3D image appears out of nowhere. But even that analogy is incomplete, because when it comes to allegorical symbolism, seeing the hidden idea does not end the job. Students now must understand a deeper point that the author is trying to convey. *Then* they must decide whether this author's point holds any water. Are the symbols soundly crafted? Are they clichéd? Relevant? Forced?

My 10th graders' first unit often centers on a book that can be seen as a clear allegory for one or more big human issues, something like *The Alchemist* or *Children of Blood and Bone*. For the endgame creative project, I want students to craft their own allegory, sometimes as a children's book and sometimes as a dystopian short story. I know, however, that most students will neither understand the core stories nor be able to write their own allegories if they don't first get to practice interpreting allegorical symbolism in some low-stakes discussions. Over the years, the following unit-opening sequence has emerged.

First, we watch a short YouTube video from the Caritas Internationalis charity organization that tells a Claymation version of Rabbi

Haim's *Allegory of the Long Spoons* (bana hayat Ver, 2014). In this silent black-and-white video, a group of emaciated figures sit around the edge of a bottomless pit, holding obscenely long spoons. In the middle of the pit is a raised platform with a bowl of food on it. With the long spoons, the people can reach the distant food just fine, but they can't then move it to their mouths. This, of course, frustrates them, and they start to fight among themselves. At the lowest point, a figure breaks their neighbor's spoon. All seems to be lost until someone thinks to use their long spoon to bring food to the recently spoonless figure. This proves to be hard work, and just as the hero's strength is about to falter, everyone else joins in and uses their own spoons to buttress the effort. The video ends with everyone happily feeding each other as it moves from grayscale to bright color and the people become nourished and happy.

At this early point in the unit, some students have just learned what a symbol is, and the term "allegory" has been defined as a "symbolic story." After watching the video once, I encourage students not to rush to decide what the entire allegory *means*. It would be helpful to first list elements in the story that seem like they might be symbolic. I say, "What do you see in the video that looks like it probably has a deeper meaning? Like it connects to real life somehow?" They respond with "The pit!" and "Those long spoons!" and "The food!" After celebrating these answers, I remind students that symbols aren't just *things* but can be *actions*, too. This usually leads them to point out the breaking of the spoon and the feeding of a neighbor. More perceptive kids point out the characters' odd refusal to use both hands. Once this list of symbols seems exhaustive, I remind them that an allegorical story cohesively uses a series of individual symbols to make a larger claim ("Like the moral of a children's book!" I say). I then ask, "So... looking at the symbols, what are some possible claims? And yes, I am saying claim*s* plural. There could be many answers—some that the author didn't even intend!" Sometimes the interpretations roll in quickly: "It's about how frustrating it is to not be able to help yourself!" and "It's about how we need to help each other to feel good!" and so on. Because this allegory is (as presented by this Claymation, at least) fairly literal, kids new to the concept get to feel good about themselves for cracking the code. I do, however, save a little special attention for kids who move past food = food and start wondering if the food could also represent other resources, like money or clean air.

From here, we move to a similar video that, again using Claymation, tells a version of Plato's famous cave allegory (Bullhead Entertainment, 2008). A group of prisoners are shackled in the depths of a cave, their bodies locked in a position where they can't turn around and see the cave's mouth. They can only see a big wall where shadows from the outside world are projected by firelight. They can't see that these massive, magnificent, and disturbing shadows are just regular people and items moving around behind them. They then create an entire mythology to justify the existence of huge monsters on the wall. One prisoner is then freed and can walk around outside. He notices what the shadows really are and hurries back to tell the other prisoners. But they can't hear him. He's now just another shadow to them.

My initial prompting works almost identically to the long spoons example. ("List the individual symbols first and what they could represent. Don't rush.") But crucially, when we get to teasing out the author's larger claims, the prompt shifts, "This cave allegory is *way* more complex than the spoons. It could be making a claim about many real-life issues. You have to take those individual symbols and then play a game of if/then. For example, *if* the shadows on the wall represent social media, *then* the claim might be...what? Turn and chat with your neighbor." We do this a few times, each ending with a partner chat. "*If* the cave represents a political party, *then* the claim might be...what?" A few seconds later, "*If* the act of leaving the cave represents leaving one's neighborhood for college or a job, *then* the claim might be...what?" I then ask for volunteers to propose *ifs* for classmates to discuss. Religion comes up often, as do romantic relationships.

After this, the discussion gently moves to literature. Children's books are great at this early stage because older students can focus on how the symbols combine to make claims and don't have to work too hard to make sense of everything else. I'm fond of using Shel Silverstein's (1964) *The Giving Tree* because it offers some of the same flexibility as the cave video. Is it about parenthood? Romantic relationships? Is it about the environment? Plus, I love how the claim is both complex and not particularly uplifting. In recent years, I have paired it with the rich Pixar short *Bao* (2018), a story about the relationship between an anthropomorphic dumpling and its human mom. After going through the same series of questions, I now ask students to "compare the claims about parental love from *The Giving Tree* to the ones in *Bao*. Where are they similar and where are they different? Which allegorical claim seems more authentic to real life?" Because this discussion prompt brings us near the top of our scaffold—if they can do this, we are probably ready to introduce our core text and get going—I think it's important to remind students that "there aren't too many 'wrong answers' when interpreting an allegory, just answers that aren't explained well enough."

Facet 5: Application

Students can effectively use and adapt what they know in new and complex contexts.

I sit to write this section having just started my 18th season coaching varsity basketball. At yesterday's practice, we spent 15 minutes drilling the specific footwork required for big men in the pick-and-roll. For the next few minutes, we drilled how ball handlers should read and navigate the action. Each player got, conservatively, at least 20 repetitions at both positions. Satisfied that everyone finally got it, we moved to a semi-live, game-like scrimmage. Gentle reader, those kids acted like they'd never seen a basketball before, much less heard of a pick-and-roll. All coaches at all levels of all sports have felt this frustration. "You *just* did this! The only thing that changed is [insert slightly different context]! Do the *same thing*!"

This is, of course, not just the coach's life. This is the core challenge of an educator's career. We spend each day teaching kids how to do a thing in one controlled context (our classrooms), in a way that encourages them to do the *same thing* later in their infinitely more complex lives. This is why well-prompted discussions are so important in this modern era. They allow us to draw consistently clear connections between formal academic ideas and real-life applications. Modern students may not be afraid that the U.S. Army will force their families to quarter soldiers. But a well-prompted discussion could help kids consider how the Third Amendment's archaic quartering restrictions might influence kids' *very* modern privacy rights. Similarly, a well-prompted discussion about rhetorical devices in *Richard III* or *Julius Caesar* can help students understand what separates political speeches that stick from those that blend into the noise.

One of the more common ways that teachers try to engage this facet of understanding is by teaching various academic theories. It's one thing for students to draw meaning from a text using only their personal preferences and experiences. It's another for them to learn how *applying* a specific framework of lenses can lead to both surprises and new interpretations. I am an ELA teacher, so this idea often means discussing established literary theories. With feminist literary theory, kids look for the power dynamics among and between genders. New historicism asks them to focus on the historical and social circumstances that influence the writing of the text. Marxist literary criticism asks students to focus on the interactions between the economic classes in a text.

Consider how Richard Wright's *Native Son*—a protest novel about racism in 1930s Chicago—could offer an opportunity for kids to apply Marxist literary criticism. Late in the story, Bigger Thomas, the book's main character and anti-hero, has been arrested for the murder of a rich White college student named Mary Dalton. As he awaits trial, the victim's father—a slumlord who made his millions exploiting families like Thomas's—surprisingly visits Thomas in jail. Mr. Dalton says, "I want you to know that my heart is not bitter. What this boy has done will not influence my relations with the Negro people. Why, only today I sent a dozen ping pong tables to the South Side Boys' Club" (p. 294). This infuriates Thomas's lawyer, who quickly shouts, "My God, man! Will ping-pong keep men from murdering?... Could *ping-pong* have kept you from making your millions? This boy and millions like him want a meaningful life, not ping-pong!" (1940, pp. 294–295). Days later, at a coroner's inquest, Thomas's lawyer again critiques Mr. Dalton's version of charity, this time chastising the victim's father on the witness stand, "So, the profits you take from the Thomas family in rents, you give back to them to ease the pain of their gouged lives and to salve the ache of your own conscience?" (p. 328).

A few prompts jump to mind here. First, students could be asked a basic question like "Let's put on our Marxist [literary theory] glasses for a second. What do we see in these scenes?" This prompt has a relatively low floor because both moments are *already* about the power dynamics between economic classes. Therefore, even students who are still developing their analytical skills will be able to give solid answers that they can be proud of. Simpler answers would be "The rich man is exploiting a poor family!" and "A gift of ping-pong tables doesn't matter when you've been stealing so much more!" A more advanced answer might sound like this: "A Marxist critic would say that charity is not automatically kind. They'd say that charity just makes people feel better about exploitative relationships and systems."

Both answers can lead to a natural pivot, where we'd ask kids to immediately take off the imaginary theoretical glasses and share if they agree with whatever theoretical takes they've pointed out. The teacher could ask, "Is that fair to Mr. Dalton? To our society?" They'd share. After students wrestle with this, we could add, "*Native Son* is a protest novel, which means that the ping-pong table donation probably has larger symbolic significance. Who are some real-world 'Mr. Daltons'? And what are some real-world 'ping-pong tables'?" Patience is important here, and many students would benefit from journaling about this prompt before volunteering to speak. Of course, *some* students think about exploitive systems often and have examples at the ready, but others do not, and we do not want their contributions to be drowned out before they are even brought to mind.

Eventually, my students tend to bring up certain charities that have questionable reputations. Some mention certain mega-corporations that have both famously horrible labor practices and million-dollar justice initiatives. Of course, a teacher should encourage students to back up their opinions with evidence. (Remember, "Show your work!") Depending on how deep a teacher wants to go, an entire project could emerge from the research needed to fully back up students' ping-pong table assertions.

A Marxist literary critique offers a low floor for this particular reading, which creates an opportunity to build most students' confidence. However, the same basic sequence of prompts would work for any other literary theory, as long as students are asked to both thoughtfully apply the lens and honestly critique its assertions. For example, a new historicist lens would consider the Red Scare when talking about how communist characters are handled in the text. A feminist lens would lead readers to wonder why the brutally murdered female characters seem dehumanized in Bigger Thomas's mind. A psychoanalytic lens would go deeper, exploring both Thomas's and Mr. Dalton's hidden thought processes and the way they justify their horrible actions. In all cases, a teacher should pivot to applying each lens's assertions to the real world and then asking kids if all those theoretical arguments make any sense on the ground.

Facet 6: Self-Knowledge

Students can effectively show metacognitive awareness, use productive habits of mind, and reflect on the meaning of the learning and experience.

Celebrity therapist Dr. Phil famously liked to ask people, "How's that working for you?" This simple question is a wonderful guidepost for the Understanding by Design framework's last facet of understanding. Our discussion prompts must regularly encourage students to reflect on their thought processes and decision making—in both their academics and beyond. Teachers know that if our students habitually reflect, they'll be more likely to move through their academic lives with intention.

Consider the sort of reflective conversation that happens after a project (or a unit of study or a school year). I tend to ask students to journal about three prompts, each with an opportunity to share. We start with "What are you proud of yourself for?" In most cases, I'll add a bit of help text to the prompt, something encouraging like, "Don't be afraid to give yourself some flowers. You know what you did well. You know where you worked hard. Don't be stingy with the self-love. Pat your back about something." Although attentive follow-up questions are *always* crucial, they are especially important when we are trying to encourage self-reflection. If a student says, "I am proud because I didn't procrastinate!" I might respond with, "Let's go!... What do you think was different about this project to make you not put it off?" If a student says, "I'm proud of the artwork on my cover!" I might say, "You *went in* on that! I saw you working on that during the work periods. It looked like it took a lot of effort! Can you describe your inspiration?" Once a student responds to the follow-up prompt, if I see a natural way to pivot to the whole class, I will say, "Did anybody else find themselves more focused this time around? Raise your hand if you did." Or "Did anyone else make a cool choice with their cover art? Raise your hand." Of course, it might be enough to happily acknowledge the hands and move on with the broad sharing. Or, if there is enthusiastic synergy with that point, I can ask a few more kids to share.

The next main reflection question is "What did you learn?" The accompanying help text might be "This can be about the content or about yourself as a writer. Or maybe something general about your work habits." The same sequence follows: first freewriting, then calling on volunteers. As volunteers share, I ask follow-up questions to push their thinking *and* show that I care enough to listen actively. Finally, when practicable, I use their responses to re-prompt their classmates, which, among other benefits, helps to strengthen the class's connective tissue. (More on this in the next section.)

The final reflection question is "If I had more time, what would I change about the project?" Although time is usually the barrier that I want to hypothetically remove, it could also be the word count. (With such large classes, all my creative projects unfortunately tend to have a restrictive word count. I tell kids that, although I will *read* the longer versions of their project, unfortunately, I can't *grade* 4,000-word stories. There isn't enough time.) This main prompt follows the same process. It's also my favorite of the bunch because I get a sneak peek of what was intended by a kid's project, even if the execution fell a little short. Plus, it models, for everyone, that it is OK to have wildly ambitious plans.

These three reflection questions are the foundation. But, of course, we can add whatever thoughtful prompts the situation inspires. For instance, if the project was more complex than a simple piece of writing, I love to add a playful "So who discovered that their tech hates them?" There is often a forest of raised hands. Many are eager to describe printers running out of ink, podcast audio not saving, and video cameras deciding to give up the ghost just as the light outside was *finally* bright enough to get the perfect shot. Among giggles, classmates express plenty of solidarity. And there is an obvious nudge from me to reflect on their planning process so that one tech fail doesn't bury them.

This final facet of understanding is clearly illustrated by this kind of post-project reflection. But our prompts can always help students develop metacognitive awareness, regardless of the type of class discussion we are having. In fact, each of the previous facets of understanding will lead us here eventually. Well-prompted discussions ultimately aid students in teasing out the greater meaning of each learning experience, a process that often helps students to better know themselves.

Techniques for Re-Prompting

Once we have set the stage with thoughtful priming prompts and followed up with well-considered core prompts, our class discussions enter their most unpredictable phase: when students *start talking.* Now is when, as the cliché goes, "All bets are off!" This moment puts our visualization to the test. How well were we able to anticipate kids' responses? Their visceral reactions? Their level of interest? And now that they are answering us—and each other—what is our role? We may not want to, as discussed in the last chapter, give up the keys, but what should we do to keep the class discussion thoughtful?

At this crucial moment, one of our most important jobs is careful re-prompting. Often, *re-prompting* refers to follow-up questions we ask immediately after a student speaks (or after students speak to each other). It can also refer to questions asked a little later in the discussion, maybe as part of a take-home essay prompt. Although strong priming and core prompts dig a strong foundation, thoughtful re-prompting ultimately keeps a discussion upright.

Here are some techniques for thoughtfully re-prompting our students.

Encourage Them

When I meet with apprentice teachers after their first discussions, we always start with the positives. Usually, they had good (albeit nervous) energy. Often, the core prompts had some potential. When we move to things to work on, the first is usually that the apprentice needs to prime the discussion better. A very close second, however, is that as students responded to prompts, the apprentice didn't acknowledge what they said. From the outside looking in, the scene can be as awkward as it sounds. In some cases, multiple exchanges went like this:

> Student: I think Jack is just evil. I don't like him.
>
> The apprentice teacher looks around the room. The student looks at the teacher and waits.
>
> Some classmates slowly, awkwardly raise their hands. The apprentice teacher calls on another student.

When I address this weirdness, the apprentice generally responds with a version of the "giving kids the keys" myth. Sometimes, they didn't fully understand what the student said. Sometimes, they admit that they were processing other information at the time, like how much time they had left in the period. Sometimes, they were just too nervous. Regardless of an apprentice's reason for not responding, I ask them to think about what their lack of response has communicated to the student (e.g., "You are wrong/boring/annoying"). The apprentice is often mortified. They often overcorrect the next class period, effusively loving the kids up after every comment. It takes a while to find an equilibrium, but they eventually get there.

A key part of this equilibrium is committing to encouraging students after they speak. Sometimes we don't want our voice to take center stage for long. In these cases, we might give kids a playfully surprised "Oh my!" after they say something unexpected. Often a "Nice!" or an "Interesting!" or a more muted "I hear you" does the trick. Much of this depends on our own natural speech patterns. I've been teased for how often I repeat, "I feel you!" In many cases, a thoughtful "Hmmm" is better than silence. Anything that communicates that, at the most basic level, we *heard* students and were interested in what they said. Sometimes, we want this encouragement to be more expansive. In these cases, we might say, "Oh, that's a *great* point." Or we can add even more. I have seen students absolutely melt after hearing me say, "Oh, that's a *great* idea! I haven't heard a kid say that in ______ years!"

On the surface, these encouraging statements aren't prompts. Although they don't ask direct questions, they still—to use the definition for "prompt" from the beginning of this chapter—"move students to action." When students feel heard, they are less likely to lose their enthusiasm for contributing.

Ask Them for Justification

This technique flows nicely from the first facet of understanding: explanation. When describing it earlier, I argued that the best core prompts ask students to show their work. Although this mission applies to our original prompt language, it also applies to our re-prompting after students start to respond. Sometimes, in the thick of a good discussion, they'll start ignoring our initial request to explain their reasoning. They might say things like "I agree" without saying what they agree *with*. They might use a term like "problematic" that they learned over social media, without saying *what* exactly about the text they found problematic. Even if they have a justification, they aren't sharing it. This could be intentional. They might not trust their own logic. Or, more commonly, they might think that their statement *needs no justification*. This, of course, is usually untrue, especially if the student has responded to a well-designed prompt. The failure to justify could also be unintentional. A student might assume that they don't have to do so because the student before them shared *their* justifications (even though their logic might be a little different). Some students just might not be used to being asked to defend their reasoning. It takes a while to get used to.

We might directly ask a student, "Why do you think that?" Sometimes a quick "Say more" works well. We might even tag this request to the last section's encouragement, something like, "Oh, I *like* that point. That's *clever*. Can you explain to your classmates where you are getting that idea from?"

A typical exchange might look like this:

> Student: I think Jack is just evil. I don't like him.
>
> Teacher: Interesting. Thanks! Sometimes people kinda like the bad guy in stories. They find something appealing about them. But you *really* don't like him, do you? I can tell in your voice. Why?

As important as it is to encourage students, it's equally important that we do not allow much slippage in our expectation that they have to show their work. A network of justifications fuels the best class discussions.

Pull Quotes and Re-Prompt

This is my favorite technique, but it depends on our success with the last one. Once we have a culture of students knowing they must justify their reasoning, we can start pulling words from these justifications and using this material to craft new prompts. Although these real-time follow-ups can be directed at the student who just spoke, they are most powerful when they are asked to the larger class. It could look like this:

> Student: I don't think Hans is such a hero for giving the Jewish man bread. He is only doing it for selfish reasons.
>
> Teacher: Interesting! Can you say why you think that?
>
> Student: He wants to be able to put his head down at night and think that he's not as bad as the rest of the Nazis. He wants to feel different. It's not about the Jewish man at all.
>
> Teacher: Whoa! Tanya says that "It's not about the Jewish man at all." What do we think about that?

With this, or something like it, our class discussion is now materially directed by a student's comment. This specific form of re-prompting is by its very nature empowering: A teacher has not only *cited* a student's thesis but has also held it up to be dissected. The class regularly does this with core texts written by published authors, but here, we are doing it with something *a kid* has to say. We might even benefit from spicing up this re-prompt with academic language.

Something like, "That's an interesting *thesis* from Tanya. It sure is an ambitious *assertion*! What do we think of it?" It's lovely to, after a few weeks or months, start hearing students use some of this same language casually in class.

Point Out Connections

This re-prompting technique takes advantage of our unique perspective as the discussion leader. As teachers, we don't have to worry about coming up with ideas. We know the content. We may also have had previous experience leading the discussion. At the very least, we have visualized the discussion. This frees up some of our brain's processing power and should enable us to better recognize connections between what students are saying. It is often helpful for us to point out these connections, not assuming students have the bandwidth or general awareness to notice them. After pointing out synergy, we can re-prompt from it. It could look like this:

> Student: I don't think Hans is such a hero for giving the Jewish man bread. He is only doing it for selfish reasons.
>
> Teacher: Interesting! Can you say why you think that?
>
> Student: He wants to be able to put his head down at night and think that he's not as bad as the rest of the Nazis. He wants to feel different. It's not about the Jewish man at all.
>
> Teacher: Whoa! That reminds me of what Mark said about the Mayor's Wife a few minutes ago! Remember that? He said that the Mayor's Wife was just trying to make herself feel better about being a Nazi by giving Liesel books! Mark didn't want to give that character any credit, and it sounds like Tanya doesn't want to give Hans any credit, either…for the same reasons! What do we think of that?

Sometimes the connections would be to certain supplementary sources—or even to core texts from earlier in the year. We are lucky if students' comments have taken us to a supplement that we've planned to use. But occasionally, we can bridge to a supplement that we—just as luckily, I'd argue—happened to have stored in our brains. Sure, unless it is a YouTube video or something else that's quickly searchable, we might not be able to show them the source *in that moment*. But we can still mention it and show them later or just ask them to look it up on their own. It could go like this:

> Student: I don't think Hans is such a hero for giving the Jewish man bread. He is only doing it for selfish reasons.
>
> Teacher: Interesting! Can you say why you think that?
>
> Student: He wants to be able to put his head down at night and think that he's not as bad as the rest of the Nazis. He wants to feel different. It's not about the Jewish man at all.
>
> Teacher: Hm. Know what that reminds me of? Did anybody see *The Help*? How about *The Blind Side*? Both have scenes where White people helped Black people in ways that people now argue were more about making themselves feel better. If any of you are curious, the real White family in *The Blind Side* just got *sued* by the Black guy they took in! Anyway, a lot of people pushed back on the idea that these characters were heroes. And it sounds like Tanya is doing the same with Hans. What do we think about that connection? Is it a stretch?

In this, and many similar cases, the teacher would not have to show students the supplement. The point of re-prompting with this sort of connection would just be to expand the parameters of the discussion. In the last chapter, I argued that discussions about broader themes often land with a bit more force. This connection allows students to critique the broad human behavior that Markus Zusak wrote about in *The Book Thief*, without being limited to the novel's Holocaust setting.

Spar with Them

This last re-prompting technique flows from the fifth facet of understanding: application. Earlier in this chapter, I described my basketball boys' slowness to apply our pick-and-roll practice to a game-like situation. This, I argued, was the core challenge of an educator's career: How do we teach students to apply what they learn in our classrooms to their more complex lives? One way is, as described earlier, to embed the challenge into our core prompts. Another way is to use re-prompting to spar with students once they've started to respond.

Rounds with a sparring partner play an important role in any boxer's training process. When the boxer is hitting a heavy bag, it doesn't hit back. A sparring partner, however, *can hit them back*. With their fists, they make it clear that the boxer won't be able to get away with certain bad habits on fight night. Yet even though good sparring partners want to tag their boxers, they do not want to hurt them. (More than a few overzealous sparring partners have been fired for trying to cause real damage in the practice ring.) They just want to help their boxer apply their skills to a new, high-stakes situation. Similarly, we can carefully spar with points that students make in our discussions, especially if they have developed the good habit of justifying their answers. The goal is not for a teacher to "win" the exchange, and it is definitely not to hurt the kids. The goal is to show them where their justifications have gotten a little thin. Sparring also helps us to show students how to defend opinions thoughtfully and with self-control. It could look like this:

> Student: I don't think Hans is such a hero for giving the Jewish man bread. He is only doing it for selfish reasons.
>
> Teacher: Interesting! Can you say why you think that?
>
> Student: He wants to be able to put his head down at night and think that he's not as bad as the rest of the Nazis. He wants to feel different. It's not about the Jewish man at all.
>
> Teacher: Gotcha. Thanks... I want to spar with you a little on that point, if that's OK.
>
> The student nods.
>
> Teacher: Cool. Two things. First, you said that Hans isn't a hero because he—and let me know if I'm saying this right, because I don't want to put words in your mouth—is "selfish." And that "he only wants to be able to put his head down at night" not feeling like a Nazi. Is that right? OK. I wonder, why is that selfish? Also, I hear a bigger point here: You seem to be saying that to be a hero, you can't think of yourself. Are you saying that? If so, why can't heroes think of themselves?

And from here, the student would be given a chance to respond to either of these related questions. When I have had versions of this exact sparring session, I'll tend to answer the student's responses only once. I don't want our back-and-forth to become theater. Nor do I want to "knock out" the student by throwing too many haymakers. (Sometimes, if it seems like I have punched too hard, I'll preemptively trouble my own argument. In this case, I might add, "I *do* get what you are saying, though. Especially in this social media age when everyone wants to take a selfie of themselves doing a good deed! Come to think of it, *multiple* religions say versions of 'do your good work in secret.' I do think you are on to something....") In the best scenario, this exchange spreads throughout the class and livens the discussion.

It can't be overstated how much good sparring depends on good relationships. Our students need to know that the exchange is not an attempt to embarrass them. It is not hostile. In many ways, it is often *fun*. Kids look forward to it. Also, this technique should not catch students by surprise. Notice that in the example, the teacher announces that they wanted to spar, then asks if it is OK. Over the course of the year, we should learn which students can be publicly sparred with this way and which shouldn't. Also, although I don't want to completely rule out sparring about particularly emotional topics, it's *often* not a good idea. We should be exceedingly careful and especially aware of the power imbalance between teachers and students. (This imbalance is also why, in the example, the teacher repeatedly asks if they are accurately representing the students' words. As an authority, we don't want to put words in kid's mouths.) If we decide to spar anyway—with the student's blessing—it still helps to remind them that we want to help them justify their thinking, and in doing so, ready them to defend their opinions in the real world.

When Should We Move On?

Every teacher has experienced *not* getting through a discussion plan. Often, we're OK with this, because our plan was flexible, and we have tomorrow to finish up. Sometimes we are less than OK because we *don't* have tomorrow. Or we realize that we'd spent too much time on the appetizers (priming prompts) and not enough on the main course (core prompts and follow-ups). In these times, it's common to wonder, "When should we have moved on from one line of questioning to another?"

In the last section, I argued that one way to re-prompt was to ask students for justification. Students' responses to this challenge can also help us to know when to move on: When students *collectively* stop justifying their answers—or seem to be in general agreement about not needing to do so—it might be time to pivot to a slightly different line of questioning.

For example, let's go back to a discussion about the bullying scene from Richard Wright's *Black Boy*. (I referenced this scene early in this chapter; in it, a young Wright's mom keeps sending him out to get groceries, even though the boy must deal with bullies on the way.) Perhaps the discussion has a moment like this:

> Teacher: With your partners, discuss whether you think that Wright's mom did the right thing. Also, try to connect whatever you say to cultural relativism, if you can!
>
> Students discuss in pairs for about three minutes, then the discussion returns to the whole class.
>
> Student: I just think it's abusive.
>
> Teacher: Why?
>
> Student: It just is.
>
> Multiple students nod.
>
> Teacher: *I think* I see a lot of agreement. Does anyone else think that Wright's mom is being abusive? Hm. OK. Let's say it *is* abusive. What would be a non-abusive way for her to handle the situation?

This teacher has decided to graciously respect the abruptness of a student's stubborn "it just is" response. There is questionable value—and considerable risk—in demanding that this student elaborate. Their refusal to engage with their teacher's "Why?" is a hint that there might be something personal going on. This teacher might even have anticipated this moment *if* they'd visualized the discussion—and any of its possible emotional trigger points—beforehand. There is no reason to deliberately set off that trip wire. The teacher has also noticed that the students' classmates don't seem that willing to follow up. It is time for this teacher to move on; here, they do so by using a quote from this student's abrupt response to craft a follow-up prompt that does not stray from the main goal of deepening the class's understanding of cultural relativism.

We might also move on from an exchange if students' responses get repetitive. This is hard, because sometimes these exchanges are entertaining or even passionate. But if we listen carefully and with enough distance, we'll realize that the students don't have anywhere meaningful to go. Let's say it goes like this:

> Teacher: OK, so do you think that Richard Wright's mom did the right thing? Why or why not? How does your answer relate to cultural relativism?
>
> Students discuss in pairs for about three minutes, then the discussion returns to the whole class.
>
> Student 1: I don't care if they're in the hood or whatever. She just made her little innocent kid act violently. She's going to have to bail him out of jail one day, and it'll be her fault.
>
> Student 2: But he doesn't get to be soft! If he's soft, he's going to be bullied his whole life.
>
> Student 1: So it's better if he just beats up anyone who gives him a hard time? Where does that lead?
>
> Student 2: Where does *being soft* lead? He's gonna get beat up every day.
>
> Student 1: Soft ain't gonna put him in jail! If he keeps acting like that, he's gonna get shot!

Students can go back and forth in this vein for *a while*. Depending on the students' personalities, the exchange could be fun to watch. It could also be terrifying, if the students don't like each other very much. But once our ears pick up that both students have stopped contributing new arguments to the exchange—and are just waiting for the other side to get tired of repeating themselves—we can move on.

Finally, we might move on when we get the feeling that the students have collectively grown bored of the exchange. Please note, despite our best efforts in whole-class discussion, we rarely have *everybody* locked in enthusiastically. By collectively, I mean the students who have already bought into the discussion through speaking or intensive listening and who now seem checked out.

This boredom might cause the repeated checking of cell phones, requests to use the bathroom, fidgeting, or hyper-focused doodling in notebooks. But there are less obvious signs that kids might be ready to move on to the next prompt. Perhaps they start chatting with their neighbors a bit more frequently or loudly than usual. Perhaps they try to engage the teacher in side conversations or raise their hands to offer up obvious non sequiturs. If we are not careful, these more social signals of boredom with an exchange might be misdiagnosed as behavior problems that require traditional discipline. It's not hard to imagine that during the aforementioned back-and-forth about *Black Boy*, a few students might switch from active listening to fiddling with their phones. Or, if the exchange is entertaining, it's not hard to imagine students chatting with their neighbors about it like they were in the front row at a sporting event. Either way, it might just be time to move on.

Good Bones

A series of good prompts works much like a skeleton beneath a high-quality class discussion. They frame a discussion. They distribute a discussion's weight appropriately among students. They cage and protect classroom relationships that we find vital. They work together to support a discussion's forward movement. A weak prompt, like a brittle bone, can shatter and cause an entire conversation to collapse onto the floor. So often, when we try to think about how class discussions have gone wrong, we understandably focus on surface issues. We analyze whether our jokes landed or whether the students seemed bored. This skin-deep analysis gives us skin-deep solutions. *Be funnier. Be more interesting.* This may be an interesting place to start, but it might lead us to frustration when we don't know what comes next.

This next step is to look beneath the surface, at the *bones* of the discussion. Did we prime the conversation thoughtfully? Were our core prompts too lengthy? Too convoluted? Did they build upon each other appropriately? Which facet of understanding were we pushing students toward? Was it the right one? Should there have been more? Did we follow up student comments sensibly? Did we stay on some exchanges for too long? These questions will not only help us but also help us to help each other. When we observe a class discussion that didn't go so well, did it still have good bones? If *not,* it's time to go back and work on strengthening our prompting, making each question more purposeful. If *so,* it may be time to consider what the next chapter has to say about what to do when class discussions, despite our best efforts, continue to stall out.

4

Keeping Deep Discussions from Stalling Out

Every dialogic teacher knows what it's like to set aside 20 minutes for a discussion that only ends up lasting 90 seconds. The eerie silence. The wandering eyes. The one kid who is doing their best to help you out but has no idea what to say. What is especially wild is that an hour earlier, the same prompt, worded the same way, could have led to 12 minutes of energetic conversation with a different class. But not with *these* kids in *this* moment.

Four Reasons Why Deep Discussions Stall Out—and What to Do Next

Over the years, I have noticed four reasons that an otherwise good class discussion may have stalled.

A Critical Number of Students Didn't Understand the Prompt

Earlier in this book, I explored the question of how hard a prompt should be. That section focused on the difficulty of a prompt's language. Here, let's address a more complex version of the question:

What should we do when not enough students initially understand what is being asked of them? (I write both "not enough" and "initially" because there are always a couple of students who need to hear their classmates engage a prompt before they fully understand it. That's both normal and OK.) Sometimes, for multiple reasons, the prompt's language was accessible, but either the larger idea or the underlying request remains obscure.

Here are some quick tips for moments like these.

First, it might be helpful to write the prompt's language on the board, preferably as we repeat it aloud. Many students, we all know, process information more smoothly when it appears visually. Of course, this is much easier for core prompts that were planned in advance. It's harder to remember to keep writing follow-up prompts as they are asked. (Apprentice teachers and students can do it, too.)

A Quick Note About Slideshows

Before moving on, a few words of advice for those of us who prefer to display a series of prompts on a slideshow, instead of writing them on the board: We should think about how many prompts we want our students to see at once. Multiple prompts, if visible, often distract students from answering whichever question the teacher wants them to engage *right now*. I saw a massive jump in my students' focus when I started setting prompts to appear individually—with a click—when the class was ready for them. As a bonus, this approach to slideshows allows teachers to build a degree of anticipation between the prompts. The added splash of unpredictability as prompts are revealed can spice up a conversation.

Also, adding an image next to a prompt might help students make sense of what has been asked of them. This is tricky, of course. We do not want to add too many confusing visual stimuli, but a visual can subtly answer questions before they are asked, giving teachers something to point to as they explain a difficult concept. More generally, this practice can stir up students' interest in the prompts or help establish a tone for the exchange that will follow.

When we notice confusion, we can also ask students to briefly chat about the prompt with their neighbors. This might seem incongruous at first—how are two confused students supposed to help each other? Although this critique makes sense, I've noticed a few benefits to the strategy. First, two confused kids *can* help each other to better understand a prompt. They might not be confused about the same thing, after all. More important, a temporary pivot to turn-and-talk gives us time to walk around and overhear what seem to be the biggest points of confusion. These little reconnaissance missions have served me well over the years.

Finally, it might help to model a possible response to the prompt. Let's say that we asked students the same symbolism question from the previous chapter, the one about Plato's cave allegory ("What do you see in the video that looks like it probably has a deeper meaning?"). In most of my classes, enough students would understand quickly enough to begin responding. But if they didn't, a teacher could model a response: "For example, you could say 'the pit.' It probably has a deeper meaning, right? After all, people don't normally eat dinner by the edge of a bottomless pit! It's strange enough to stand out, which probably means that it's meant to grab the viewer's attention. Can anyone else think of something else that *stands out*? Maybe because it is weird and out of place?" This modeling might offer students enough of a foothold to engage the prompt.

Many of us might instinctively do this when our students appear confused by our prompt. But we mustn't go too far. Helpful modeling can quickly turn into a mind-numbing monologue. We model one possible answer, then another with a slight variation, then rephrase the question, then answer the rephrase, and on and on. Earlier in this book, when writing about how long a prompt should be, I reminded teachers to let students "focus on one thing at a time." There, I was talking about asking too many different questions at once, but the same idea applies here, too. The more we talk, the more we tax kids' working memories. Plus, once they determine that their teacher is about to do all the analytical work for them, there is no urgent need for kids to remain focused on the prompt.

Students Didn't Do the Reading

I began my teaching career at a school where, for many reasons both in and outside their control, a lot of students struggled to come to class. This means that, on any given day, I had no idea which students would be there. I could plan few, if any, discussions around an assumption that the same students who were there yesterday would be there today. (This also meant that few valued resources like books went home with kids, because our school was not particularly confident that it would ever get them back.) So every discussion had to make sense within the context of a single class period. I could neither assume prior knowledge about a text or depend on the ability to follow up with a student the next day. This is no longer my teaching reality, but I learned a career-shaping lesson about class discussions that first year: *Always* be ready for *nobody* to have done the reading.

Practically, this means that class discussions benefit from teachers giving students immediate access to relevant information and key terms before we start prompting. Some kids might not need this information, as they came to the moment prepared. Others, for whatever reason, did not, and so we face the choice either to leave them behind or to give them *just enough* of a grounding to participate. If our pride gets involved, we might choose the former. This is understandable. But it too often is an illogical choice. If students do not have enough information to participate, awkward silence might not be the only consequence. These kids might become a classroom management problem. And what's the point? It's not like students who enter a conversation unprepared will suddenly start doing their homework tonight out of embarrassment.

There are a few ways to give students just enough information to participate. All of them eat valuable discussion time, so we must choose wisely. One option is to read aloud the portion of the text that will be discussed. If we want the class to discuss one moment in an entire scene, we could read aloud just that moment, even if it's only one paragraph in 25 assigned pages of homework. (I am a fan of making these readings interactive, by having kids act out or do dramatic voices.) This read-aloud is not just for the kids who didn't read. It's for the kids who read while doing their chores, playing video games, or watching TV. It's for the kids who read at 2 a.m. with their eyes half-closed or in the lunch period before class. Everyone could always use a review. Any veteran ELA or history teacher can remember students gasping at something that happened in the reading, and when asked why they are surprised, saying a version of "I swear that I read! I didn't remember that happening!" As mentioned earlier in the book, I teach students *Lord of the Flies*. Every year, when Simon dies, students who have not read attentively are surprised as I read the passage aloud, "At once the crowd [of kids]... poured down the rock, leapt on the beast [Simon], screamed, struck, bit, tore. There were no words, and no movements but the tearing of teeth and claws" (Golding, 1954, p. 153). They say, "Wait, they *ate* him?" Giggling, I say, "In a way, yup!" And suddenly, the kids are *locked in*.

Although a read-aloud can take a few minutes, a quick summary might only take a few seconds. It might even help to dramatically sell the reading. Something as simple as "So in last night's reading, ______ got in an argument with ______ and it was wild!" After saying something like this, we might face another choice: tell the class what happened or ask for volunteers to do so. It might be tough to figure out which to do. If we ask for volunteers, there could be an awkward silence, which, admittedly, isn't always bad. Sometimes students just need time to think or to work up the courage to raise their hands. However, these silences *can* be needlessly destructive when they follow simple requests, like asking students what happened in the reading. We face the temptation to passive-aggressively extend the silence, thinking we are embarrassing unprepared students. And I've seen students do the same, wanting to punish an overeager teacher. And again, what's the point? If we don't get a quick answer, we should just tell them what happened! Now we can ask our interesting prompts and get going.

Just to be clear, I am not against accountability. I'm pretty old-school about quizzes, using them for just about every take-home reading. Students who do not do the reading will fail these quizzes. Students who don't do the reading will write bad essays. They will probably not get a good grade in my class. But *class discussions* have to be different. *Everyone* gets to engage with the ideas, if they have even the slightest motivation to do so. Kids who didn't read might not get as much out of a conversation as kids who did. But they should get *something*. Put simply, great class discussions should give students who are less motivated by grades a reason to read. It's a similar feeling to a friend making us watch an episode of their favorite HBO series. We need just enough basic information to root ourselves in the episode that we are watching. And if that episode is entertaining enough, we're more likely to watch future episodes. We might just go home and stream the show from the beginning.

Students Reacted to a Text—or Our Prompt—Much Differently Than We Expected

Sometimes we are certain that our students will find a text—or our prompt—funny. And they do not. Even more awkwardly, we expect students to be emotionally moved by a text or prompt. And they are not. In trickier situations, a group of students will react to a text or prompt in wildly different ways, when we expected a fairly uniform emotional response.

For instance, I tend to end units that engage the Holocaust by showing *Defiance* (2008), a movie loosely inspired by a famous Jewish resistance movement in Eastern Europe during World War II. Generally, students enjoy the action and appreciate my prompts about the various ethical dilemmas that the characters face in the film. A few years ago, however, a student approached me in the middle of the film to ask that I tell students to stop laughing. I was a little confused, but then I noticed what this kid was talking about. Classmates were pretty much acting like they would in a movie theater. Saying "Ooh!" and elbowing each other during big scenes (like when the protagonist got revenge on a Nazi collaborator). This behavior carried over to when we paused the film to discuss it. I had not thought much of it, but this student, who was Jewish, felt that the behavior was disrespectful. They'd expected a generally somber, contemplative mood as classmates watched and discussed the text, and these classmates were treating it like any entertainment media. This frustrated this student, which caused them to disengage. Classmates picked up on, and were turned off by, this frustration.

I have felt similarly when discussing issues near and dear to my heart. One of the slideshows that I use to teach and discuss life in the Jim Crow South includes a photo of a lynching. Typically, students gasp. Some avert their eyes. These are expected responses. But sometimes a few students giggle nervously. Once or twice, sporadic giggling has caused a conflict between students. (More on managing conflict in the next section.) Sometimes, I get the same responses from literary content during a big scene in the text that students *should* find sad. But they do not react in ways that most people translate as sadness.

There is no easy solution, mostly because, honestly, it might be an overreach to consider these unexpected responses to be a problem. Students are different, and they react to both texts and the prompts that we create about them in their own ways. This is why, in the last chapter, I suggested that we focus on one or more facets of understanding. The goal of a discussion isn't to make students react in a certain visceral way. It's to help them *figure something out*—even if that something is empathy. We can't let ourselves be pushed too far off course by unexpected student reactions.

Of course, we can notice patterns in students' visceral responses and then use this information to make decisions. We can say, "Hey, too many students laughed at that. It was distracting. Let's use a different supplementary source next year." We can say, "That prompt ruined the vibe. Now it's depressing in here. I've got to tweak it before the next period comes in." Similarly, we can use these unexpected student reactions to check the status of our classroom community. If it feels like students don't care at all about how their reactions are being perceived by vulnerable classmates, maybe it is time to go back to the "will to strengthen relationships" reminder and reinvest some time in community building, because the moment is showing cracks in our communal foundation.

A Conflict Between Students Has Become Unproductive

Somewhere, somehow, it has all gone wrong. Our feistiest students are at each other's throats, while classmates look at the fracas and back to us with eyes that plead, "Do something!" If only we had the slightest idea what to do. Ten minutes ago, we were discussing a juicy book passage, a complex time period, or a spicy current event. Sure, we'd known that this discussion could rankle. A part of us was even tempted to skip it (right now, we wish we did). Five minutes ago, against our better judgment, we'd called on that sometimes snarky kid who said something her classmate did not appreciate. The frustration was shared. Battle lines were drawn quicker than we'd imagined possible. Thirty seconds ago, flailing for a toehold, we'd threatened discipline. Or maybe we'd weighed in on the side we think makes the most sense, hoping to squash the conflict with the brute force of our authority. Whichever option we chose, it didn't work. The discussion is ruined. And a quick glance at our watch shows that there are *gasp* 20 minutes left in class!

Most dialogic teachers have been here (or adjacent to here). Though we should start our discussion planning with visualization, we can never, with full certainty, predict exactly what students are going to say. This is doubly true when discussing the most sensitive issues in a text or our world. Many of us have thought that we understood a student's cultural background and values and that we had a feel for their personality or current mood, only for them to react to a classmate's take on an issue with surprisingly raw emotion. A debate then becomes an argument. The former, when well executed, is both scholarly and productive. The latter, at best, is a waste of everyone's time. At worst, it corrodes the threads that bind our classroom community, maybe even permanently.

So how do we get our class discussions back on track from an unproductive student conflict? This situation is too complex for absolutes, but here are a few pro tips.

First, it might make sense to re-prompt from the middle of the unproductive argument's Venn diagram. By this, I mean that we could find a point where the students agree, and re-prompt from there. Imagine a conversation about the NFL player Colin Kaepernick's decision to kneel during the national anthem in 2016. In a YouTube video that I use often during workshops with fellow educators, a Kansas teacher asks students, "Was Colin Kaepernick right or wrong?" (SM East Harbinger, 2016). This binary question, for reasons already explained in this book, is unlikely to be useful. But with a topic like this, it can be unintentionally destructive. Answering it, hypothetical Student 1 might say, "If he doesn't like it here, he can just leave." Affronted, Student 2 might respond, "Why should a Black man like this racist country?" In a blink, the conversation becomes stalled by an unproductive exchange; Student 1 names things the United States has done for Black people, while Student 2 talks classmates through a lowlight reel of homegrown racist policies. This could go on for *a while,* and in many classrooms, including mine, it has.

Instead of continuing this repetitive exchange or abruptly ending the discussion, we could pivot to a broader discussion about the First Amendment to the U.S. Constitution, which all students tend to support (in one way or another). From here, we might ask, "Can a successful protest movement *ever* be inoffensive?" As the students are being challenged to "show their work" in justifying their answers, we can follow up with versions of "What's the historical relationship between protest movements and the First Amendment?" We might not have resources at the ready for students to peruse, but frankly, most teachers should have enough of a knowledge base about this history of protest movements to give a few historical examples on the fly. (If we don't, we probably were not equipped to lead students in a Kaepernick conversation. At least not that day!) Alternatively, we could ask students, "How does the First Amendment protect us in the workplace? How should it be balanced against the desires/needs of an employer?" Again, this gives us the chance to pivot to supplementary sources, even if we need to show them to students the next day.

Of course, all these prompts are better than the original binary "Is Colin Kaepernick right or wrong?" The *next* time we discuss the issue, we could certainly start with these better, more rigorously academic questions. Instead of just asking kids to repeat and argue over whatever politics they hear at the dining room table or on social media, we can lead a fruitful discussion about relevant case law. With proper background, we might even be able to ask questions like "How has the Supreme Court defined *protected speech*? Do you agree with this definition? Why?"

I have one more tip for dealing with conflicts: We should plan discussions that *analyze* society's larger fights, instead of merely *re-creating* them. For example, let's say we are discussing the more violent protests that emerged in 2020. We may have, unwisely, asked students if it was permissible to destroy property when protesting. (Again, a binary prompt sets us up to be less productive.) Student 1 might respond with "There is never an excuse for destroying people's property!" Student 2 could counter that "property is not more important than Black lives!" Both viewpoints could be backed up by personal experiences. Student 1's family might own a store. Student 2's cousin may have been murdered by the police. If you were teaching in 2020, you heard versions of this exchange, even if it wasn't in your classroom.

We could let the students just go back and forth, mimicking the unproductive exchanges that they see from adults in the outside world. Or we could pivot to a discussion about historical protest movements that are *less recent,* and therefore *less raw*: the LA riots in 1992, the Watts riots in 1965, all the way back to the Boston Tea Party in 1773. We could ask a version of "How effective have historical protest movements been when they have included the destruction of property? Why?" or "What is the philosophy of nonviolent direct action? How is it similar/different from 'any means necessary' philosophies? What might make one method of protest work better than another in specific situations?" Again, we have moved from a needless point-scoring argument where neither party is likely to change their minds to a rigorous, if still passionate, class discussion.

Early in this book, I wrote that it's not enough for kids to just share their opinions. I then argued that all great class discussions require *inquiry.* Students have got to be figuring something out. This is especially true when they are discussing controversial issues. Unproductive arguments will cause some of these discussions to stall. It happens to the best of us. We've all got to get good at guiding students back towards inquiry, which will lead us to more productive exchanges.

Generative AI: An Unreliable Guide

I want to highlight one more reason why teachers' class discussions might stall out: We might have not crafted the discussion prompts ourselves. In this era, we may have even used generative artificial intelligence (AI) to craft discussion prompts for us.

It is understandable that we would do so. Generative AI tools make many aspects of our teaching practice more efficient. These tools can draft lesson plans and assignment sheets. They can draw elucidative graphics for slide decks and write the accompanying copy. While a few years ago, it might have taken an entire weekend to collate all the information needed to make an introductory slideshow, with the help of generative AI, we can make a gorgeous and informative presentation in the minutes between *Sunday Night Football* and bedtime. So of course it makes sense for teachers to ask generative AI tools to write our discussion prompts for us.

But what might be the consequences in doing so? In 2023, ASCD invited me to speak at ISTE's annual conference, which was conveniently held in my hometown of Philadelphia. I knew that this conference would attract teachers who were generally more open to AI-powered teaching tools, which would make them the perfect group to join me in an experiment that I'd been eager to try for weeks: asking generative AI—in this case, ChatGPT—to craft discussion prompts for difficult classroom discussions. How useful would the language model's suggestions be right out of the box? How much work would need to be done after the initial prompting to make the prompts ready? And, most important to me, what interesting patterns emerged with the sort of discussion prompts that generative AI suggested?

The session began with participants asking the AI to "generate 10 classroom discussion prompts for a [insert grade level] classroom discussion about [insert a contemporary controversial issue]." Participants could fill in the blanks, but I offered a few examples of what I meant by controversial: topics where there is a great public disagreement, like the January 6 insurrection, the Black Lives Matter movement, transgender rights, and the *Dobbs* decision. As the AI-suggested prompts emerged on their screens, I asked participants to look for advantages and disadvantages to each one. How would their current students react to them? After some note taking, they discussed it with their neighbors.

Then we repeated the process by asking Chat GPT a slightly different question, "Generate 10 classroom discussion prompts for a [grade level] classroom discussion about [historical event or a book with controversial themes]." Although the first exercise asked the AI to help us discuss a hot-button current event, this one was meant to find prompts for tackling a thorny text.

The ensuing conversation with teachers was fascinating. I told them that my goal was to neither denigrate nor lionize AI lesson-planning tools. We just wanted to tinker around and see what happened. ChatGPT suggested some prompts that blew teachers' minds and some that made us giggle and roll our eyes.

I then revealed that I had spent the previous few days doing the same activity dozens of times, looking for any consistent patterns—both beneficial and troublesome—with AI-suggested prompts. I chose three books from my curriculum that I am intimately familiar with (and cite often in this book): *Lord of the Flies*, *Native Son*, and *Born a Crime*. I also asked ChatGPT to craft discussion prompts about a controversial current event: President Donald Trump's speech at the Ellipse on January 6, 2021. I welcome curious readers to conduct the same experiment, with any modern generative AI tool.

In my experiments, generative AI had some consistently beneficial habits. For example, ChatGPT was surprisingly good at linking a thorny text to a real-world context. Yet far more interesting to the group at ISTE, and useful in this chapter, are the *less* beneficial habits that I repeatedly noticed in my experiments, habits that might cause our discussions to stall out and crash. I saw each of the following issues multiple times.

Generative AI Might Ask Inaccurate or Misleading Prompts

For example, I asked ChatGPT for questions about Chapter 1 of *Born a Crime*. The AI model suggested, "Discuss the significance of the story about the DJ named Hitler in Chapter 1. What does it reveal about the power of names and the influence of pop culture in shaping perceptions and attitudes?" The DJ named Hitler appears toward the end of the book, not Chapter 1. And even if he did, that very complex and *very* sensitive passage has nothing to do with pop culture.

Similarly, I asked about Chapter 1 of *Lord of the Flies*. The AI offered, "Analyze the interactions between the boys and their gradual descent into savagery in Chapter 1. What factors contribute to the breakdown of social norms?" This is a silly question, as the boys' "descent into savagery" doesn't happen until later in the book. In fact, early on, they famously cling to societal norms, like voting for a leader and assigning jobs.

Hey, all teachers occasionally get facts wrong. However, when we've made a factual error ourselves, we are usually able to notice where we went awry and course correct. But when a factual error is tucked in among more legitimate-sounding prompts—none of which we crafted ourselves—we might not notice it until we've already put it before students. Multiple issues then arise. First, when the issue is as sensitive as the *Born a Crime* Hitler example, we might end up hurting students by engaging a topic haphazardly. Second, because we are the authority, students might incorrectly think that *they've* misunderstood the text, when it was the AI. Third, when the mistake is obvious, we just look sloppy, like we don't know the course material or haven't prepared. All these issues can bring a conversation to a standstill.

Generative AI Might Create Prompts That Are Academic-Sounding but Nonsensical

For example, I asked for questions about *Native Son*. It suggested, "Explore the role of Bigger's family in Part 1. How do his relationships with his mother, brother, and sister contribute to the dynamics within the Thomas household?" This sounds nice, but it essentially asks students a circular "How do Bigger's family relationships contribute to... his family relationships?" I am not sure what students are supposed to say in response to a question like this.

Similarly, when I asked about *Born a Crime*, it offered, "Discuss the role of storytelling and oral tradition in *Born a Crime*. How does Trevor Noah use storytelling not only as a form of entertainment but also as a means of preserving and sharing cultural experiences?" Yes,

Noah's memoir, like all memoirs, tells a lot of stories. Yes, it takes place in Africa, a continent steeped in rich oral storytelling traditions. Yes, stand-up comedy, which Noah eventually made a career out of, can be considered part of an oral storytelling tradition. But the actual text of *Born a Crime* does not richly discuss the way that the oral tradition is used to preserve cultural experiences. It also doesn't cover Noah's stand-up career. To be frank, the AI asked this question because *Born a Crime* takes place in Africa—a place that famously has a tradition of griots—and is a memoir. It sounds nice, culturally competent even, but it would lead to an obvious dead end.

These nonsensical questions stall out conversations because students never quite know what is being asked. Sometimes, because the questions *sound* rigorous and use academic language, students might even attribute their confusion to their own perceived lack of intellect. At the very least, it makes them doubt how much they understood the reading. Or the lab. Or the historical source. This blow to students' confidence might not deal permanent damage, but it might be enough to convince a few kids that they don't know enough about the content to participate that day.

Generative AI Creates Many Prompts with Leading Language

For example, Chat GPT suggested this prompt about *Native Son*: "Bigger Thomas is often seen as the product of his environment. How does the setting of the South Side of Chicago contribute to his mindset and actions? Analyze the influence of poverty, lack of opportunities, and social inequality on Bigger's character development." This prompt starts strong, but in the last sentence gives students only three acceptable answers: poverty, lack of opportunities, and social inequality.

ChatGPT behaved similarly when asking students to make sense of symbolism. Of the same novel, it suggested that I ask students to "Explore the symbolism of the rat in Part One. What does the rat represent in Bigger's life, and how does it reflect his feelings of powerlessness and entrapment? Discuss the roles of fear and violence associated with the rat imagery." If this prompt had stopped after "Explore the symbolism of the rat in Part One," students would then have the freedom to, well, *explore* said symbolism. But instead of encouraging such exploration, the AI often answers its own questions. This isn't help text. It is telling students that *the* answer is "powerlessness and entrapment" followed by "fear and violence." But what if students wanted to say something else? And crucially, what are kids supposed to say, even if they agree with the provided answer? There is now little to discuss, because the AI has solved its own problem! This over-guidance (in lieu of help text) is an understandable mistake, one that human teachers make often. So often, in fact, that it seems to have influenced the plethora of data that AI tools are trained on.

Generative AI Seems Hesitant to Generate Prompts About Specific Quotations in a Text

For example, I asked the AI to generate discussion prompts to help students analyze President Donald Trump's speech at the Ellipse on January 6, 2021. It suggested, "Conduct a close textual analysis of Trump's speech on January 6. Identify key rhetorical devices such as repetition, appeals to emotion, or other persuasive techniques." I had to re-prompt the AI language model multiple times before its questions began to engage direct quotes from President Trump's speech. Even then, the questions were bland. ("President Trump said, 'We love you. You're very special.' What effect does this expression of love and specialness have on the audience?")

If we are not careful, this reluctance to cite specific quotes will nudge class discussions away from being academically rigorous. When the AI asks students to look at a text as a whole, they are less likely to ground their reasoning in specific parts of the text. Throughout this book, I've repeated how important it is that our prompts ask students to show their work. Students learn to do this partially because good prompts pull sections that are ripe for detailed textual analysis. Breaking down, interpreting, and sometimes debating the meaning of a *specific quote* (rather than debating a whole text or general concept) gives a class discussion a practical chance to be productive. If the AI is unwilling to do this, it might set our class discussion up for failure.

* * *

Most of these flaws can be mitigated by a simple procedure: asking ourselves how *we* would answer if we were asked the AI prompt. As talented professionals who know our subject matter, we shouldn't find ourselves thoroughly stumped by a discussion prompt meant for children. We shouldn't have to read its language five times before we realize what part of a text the question is referencing. We should be able to not only answer the question but also imagine how our hypothetical classmates would. Then we should be able to visualize a thoughtful exchange of ideas between all of us.

AI tools (or any scripted curriculum for that matter) *can* be useful, especially as they remove the terror of planning from a blank page. It might even provide excellent priming or core prompts that we wouldn't have thought of. It *certainly* saves time. But crucially, AI will not help us craft our follow-up prompts, which depend on student responses. These follow-ups, which were discussed at the end of the last chapter, make up the bulk of any great class discussion. AI tools can't help, because they do not know how our very human students have responded to its initial questions.

Not only are AI tools unable to help us respond to real-time comments, but they also don't know our students. We do. And as we lead similar conversations for the second, fifth, or twentieth time, we can develop an even better idea of which student answers to be prepared for. We will have heard the jokes. We will have navigated the minefields. We will have learned which student tangents are worth following. Most important, we will know where our students have been confused in the past and how to best assist them. All this experience goes into the careful crafting and sequencing of our prompts—and we should commit to the productive struggle of doing so. (Then, maybe, check to see if the AI tools have any *extra* cool stuff to offer.)

It Happens!

Sometimes class discussions stall out. They fall flat. The students don't understand us. They don't do the reading. They react unexpectedly to the text or prompt. They get into unanticipated arguments. We might get prompts from elsewhere, thinking that we will be ready for our students' responses to them, but we aren't. One of the best lessons that I learned from my educator mom was to throw *short* pity parties. We have a right to be a bit grumpy when a thoughtfully designed discussion stalls. But much of our longevity in this career comes down to shrugging, saying to ourselves, "It happens!" and pushing forward. We must try and not let a discussion that has stalled due to something outside our immediate control undermine the *next* discussion.

Stalled discussions can be a jumping-off point for good collaborative PD. We can ask each other, "What do you think happened here? It worked with the other class." We can ask colleagues if they have developed a system for handling any of the issues that I've brought up in this chapter. And if nothing else, we can remind each other that we are not soothsayers or prophets. We cannot predict with 100 percent certainty how each of our classroom moves will influence a discussion. Hiccups happen. We can just keep gathering information, tweaking our approach, and getting right back into the mix.

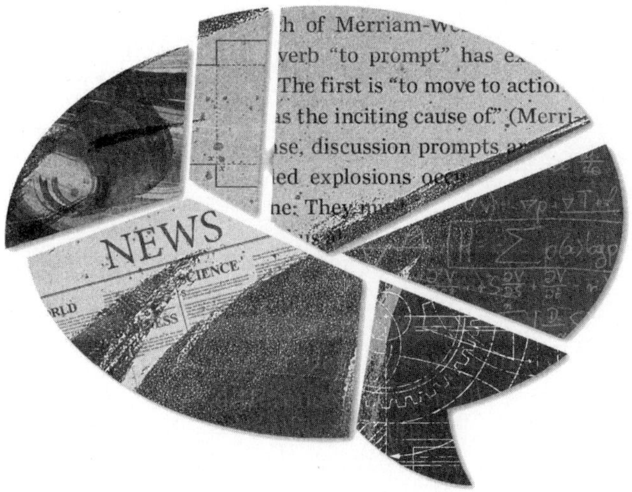

Part II

Exercises for Professional Development

We learn our most important lessons about teaching the hard way, and learning how to write discussion prompts is no different. The feedback is often immediate. We ask a question, and the students don't respond. We frown and think, "Well, that didn't work." We ask a question, and 15 hands shoot into the air. We smile, and think, "Whew! I hope I remember *exactly* what I said next period." We ask a question, and our students start fighting. We gasp and think, "OK, I need to *never* do that again." And discussion after discussion, year after year, this process builds and shapes our dialogic toolkit. This book has not offered ways to skip this laborious process. In it, I've merely shared some of the prompting language that I use, along with the reasoning that supports each decision. Hopefully, in quoting my specific syntax and diction, I have also provided a rough set of guided notes, where readers can fill in the blanks to craft their own prompts.

Part II offers readers a low-stakes chance to practice the prompting strategies introduced and modeled in this book. Each section will start with an excerpt of academic content and its general context. Full disclosure: Most of the following example texts have been used in my high school ELA and humanities classrooms, across all four grades. Instead of creating a few hypothetical examples from other disciplines, I have interviewed a few trusted colleagues to get examples from their classrooms. With each example, readers will be invited to craft discussion prompts. Finally, I will share the prompts that I have used over the years, with generally beneficial results.

Before we start, I have to make three things clear.

First, your goal is *not* to guess what I—or my colleagues—would do. Our students are not your students. We are coming to the text with different background knowledge. We may have slightly different goals for the conversation. Imagine, instead, that we are two colleagues sitting side by side at a professional development session, sharing best practices. I am showing you what I do, you are sharing what you would do, and hopefully we can find something to steal from each other! (I *would* love to hear your ideas. My contact info isn't hard to find online.)

Second, I rarely ask my students *all* of the core prompts that appear in these exercises in any one class conversation. For each of the following discussions, I merely give a sampling of prompts that I have used in the past—focusing on those that have led to the most fruitful exchanges between kids.

Third, remember that much of a class discussion's value lies in the follow-up prompts that we ask after students start responding to a core prompt. I will try to share *some* of the ways that I build upon the most common student responses, but I do not want to try to cover every possible thing a kid could say. Too much of that, and this part of the book turns into a piece of creative writing, which might not be particularly useful in the long run. You can trust, then, that all student responses are the authentic words of 14- to 18-year-old students in Mr. Kay's ELA class—and the classes of my colleagues—at Science Leadership Academy in Philadelphia, Pennsylvania.

The Lord of the Flies

By William Golding
Chapter 1, pages 22–23

The Context

Grade Level and Discipline: 10th grade ELA

The Unit's Goals: Students will better understand allegorical storytelling by analyzing *The Lord of the Flies* and writing their own allegorical stories.

At This Point in the Text: A group of pre-teen boys have crash landed on what they are discovering to be a deserted island. Readers have met Ralph, who is athletic and handsome, and a boy they call Piggy, who is overweight and socially awkward. They have found a conch shell and have discovered that blowing into it makes a huge sound. They've used this sound to call the other boys over to their location. One of the groups that comes over is a choir, who has a leader named Jack. Jack is redheaded and described as being "ugly without silliness." In this excerpt, the boys are deciding who will be their leader as they try to get rescued.

The Excerpt

> Jack spoke.
>
> "We've got to decide about being rescued."
>
> There was a buzz. One of the small boys, Henry, said that he wanted to go home.
>
> "Shut up," said Ralph absently. He lifted the conch. "Seems to me we ought to have a chief to decide things."
>
> "A chief! A chief!"
>
> "I ought to be chief," said Jack with simple arrogance, "because I'm chapter chorister and head boy. I can sing C sharp."
>
> Another buzz.
>
> "Well then," said Jack, "I—"
>
> He hesitated. The dark boy, Roger, stirred at last and spoke up. "Let's have a vote."
>
> "Yes!"

> "Vote for chief!"
>
> "Let's vote—"
>
> This toy of voting was almost as pleasing as the conch. Jack started to protest but the clamor changed from the general wish for a chief to an election by acclaim of Ralph himself. None of the boys could have found good reason for this; what intelligence had been shown was traceable to Piggy while the most obvious leader was Jack. But there was a stillness about Ralph as he sat that marked him out: there was his size, and attractive appearance; and most obscurely, yet most powerfully, there was the conch. The being that had blown that, had sat waiting for them on the platform with the delicate thing balanced on his knees, was set apart.
>
> "Him with the shell."
>
> "Ralph! Ralph!"
>
> "Let him be chief with the trumpet-thing."
>
> Ralph raised a hand for silence.
>
> "All right. Who wants Jack for chief?"
>
> With dreary obedience the choir raised their hands.
>
> "Who wants me?" Every hand outside the choir except Piggy's was raised immediately. Then Piggy, too, raised his hand grudgingly into the air.

What Would You Ask Your Students?

____

____

____

____

____

____

____

____

____

What Do I Usually Ask My Students?

1. When Ralph suggests that they need a chief, Jack says, "I ought to be chief... because I'm chapter chorister and head boy. I can sing C sharp" (p. 22). Are being chapter chorister and head boy relevant additions to Jack's leadership application? Do those things matter? *Some students say yes, some no. I push the no kids*

to justify their reasoning, and we eventually agree that Jack's prior leadership experience is probably useful.

2. Is Jack's ability to sing C-sharp important to being a leader? *Students: "No!" This time, we generally agree. Often there is some laughter, and with it, an opportunity to sprinkle in some playfulness by asking, "Who here can sing C-sharp?" Some students will want to share goofy reasons why singing talent is actually relevant to leadership, and it's perfectly fine to lean into the fun.*
3. William Golding seems to be making an argument about irrelevant leadership qualifications that some people find important. What are some leadership qualifications from the real world that are as irrelevant as Jack's ability to sing C-sharp? *Students, after a little bit of journaling and time to think, often say, "How much money they have!" and "Their race!" and "Their gender!" and "How many social media followers they have!" and so on. I gently ask each respondent to justify why the qualification is not actually that relevant for a leadership position. Sometimes there are minor debates over particular examples, but nothing too intense. The only real point here is to have students practice making symbolic connections to the real world.*
4. Let's read that last paragraph again. Any volunteers? *We read from "This toy of voting" to "The being that had blown that, had sat waiting for them on the platform with the delicate thing balanced on his knees, was set apart"* (p. 22). Golding seems to be using this moment to argue that humans foolishly tend to choose the most attractive people to lead us. I get where he's coming from, but I have to tell you that I kind of disagree. It's something that feels true, but I don't know if there is much evidence that backs it up! Here, pull out your phones. Look at the presidents of the United States. *The kids usually start giggling.* I don't see too many models being picked to be the leader of the free world! What do you think about Golding's argument? Does it hold water? *Students turn and talk about this one for a while before going to whole class. Some students agree passionately with Golding; some do not. Some point out that there are different kinds of leadership where attractiveness is important. Others*

argue, interestingly, that attractiveness might not matter for men, but it does for women. As always, I ask for students to explain their reasoning.

5. It says, "Every hand outside the choir except Piggy's was raised immediately. Then Piggy, too, raised his hand grudgingly into the air" (p. 23). Why did Piggy hesitate to raise his hand? *Students often answer that Piggy was being shy. When I ask them to explain, kids discover that the text doesn't really support their analysis. Piggy doesn't have too much trouble opening his mouth. With more time to think, my students tend to say that Piggy was waiting his turn to be nominated. When this didn't happen, he grudgingly agreed to vote for Ralph.* How often, in the real world, do qualified people choose to support leaders who are less qualified? *This exchange is not as important as the one before it, but it does have some staying power. I return to this moment a few times throughout* Lord of the Flies*—as the characters' little island society falls apart—asking my students if lives would have been saved if Piggy had cared to make a case for himself as leader.*

Far from the Tree

By Robin Benway
GRACE, pages 7–8

The Context

Grade Level and Discipline: 9th grade ELA

The Unit's Goals: Students will better understand the value of perspective through analyzing *Far from the Tree* and writing their own multinarrative stories.

At This Point in the Text: This is the beginning of a multinarrative novel about three teenage half-siblings that meet each other for the first time. The author takes turns telling the story from each half-sibling's perspective. The first character that readers meet is named Grace. She is a senior in high school. Readers at this moment are learning that Grace had a baby earlier in the year. She calls this baby "Peach." Readers will also find out within the next few pages that Grace then gave Peach up for adoption and that Grace herself was adopted when she was a baby.

The Excerpt

> When school had started up that year, Grace hadn't gone back with everyone else. She was too pregnant, too round, too exhausted. Also, there was the risk of her going into labor one day during AP Chem and traumatizing everyone in the junior class. She wasn't exactly disappointed by this decision. By the time summer vacation had rolled around, she had grown tired of feeling like a sideshow freak, people giving her so much room in the hallways that she couldn't remember the last time anyone had touched her, even accidentally.
>
> Peach was born at 9:03 p.m. on homecoming night, right when Max was being crowned homecoming king because, Grace thought bitterly, boys who get girls pregnant are heroes and girls who get pregnant are sluts. Leave it to Peach to steal Max's thunder, though. The first thing Grace's daughter ever did and it was genius. She was so proud. It was like Peach knew she was the heir to the throne and had arrived to claim her tiara.
>
> Peach came out of her like fire, like she had been set aflame. There was Pitocin and white-hot pain that seared Grace's spine and ribs and hips into rubble. Her mother held her hand and wiped her hair back from her

sweaty forehead and didn't mind that Grace kept calling her Mommy, like she had when she was four years old. Peach twisted and shoved her way through her, like she knew that Grace was just a vessel for her and that her real parents, Daniel and Catalina, were waiting outside, ready to take Peach home to her real life.

Peach had places to be, people to see, and she was done with Grace.

What Would You Ask Your Students?

What Do I Usually Ask My Students?

1. What do you think might be some of the challenges that authors (like Robin Benway) face when writing books (like *Far from the Tree*) meant to engage teenagers? Both Benway and I were teens in the mid- to late '90s. Cell phones had just arrived, and social media was still years away. What might be tough about someone our age writing a realistic modern teenage story? *Many students, cued by the help text, talk about the impact of social media. Some students share perceived social differences: They think that teens back in the '90s were less politically engaged, less "woke," and so on. We kick this assertion around a bit. I tend to agree with them on this but jokingly push back at assertions that we were somehow purer back in the day.*
2. Let's reread the paragraph on page 7 that starts with "Peach was born..." When reading this and remembering my own teenage years back in the '90s, the statement, "boys who get girls pregnant are heroes and girls who get pregnant are sluts" seems only partly realistic. I do know that slut-shaming is a

very real and horrible thing. But that first part doesn't match my lived experience. I've never seen a boy get someone pregnant and have his boys high-fiving him saying, "Good job!" It's always "Oh, you messed up!" Does the part about high school boys seem accurate from your experience? *Students tend to answer with high energy, especially as I openly invite them to disagree with me. Sometimes they say that Benway has it right and argue that she must have done her research on modern high school experiences. Sometimes students agree with me, saying that the author may not be accurately capturing real life. (Every year, a few students need to be patiently reminded that I am not disputing Benway's slut-shaming assertion. I take special care to assure students that this form of misogyny is rampant, wrong, and unfortunately timeless.) Crucially, throughout the book, we return to versions of the core prompt: "Does Benway have this right? Is this how teens act/think/talk?" Students enjoy continually tracking Robin Benway's relative successes at writing for young people.*

3. Remember how we talked about "Mirrors, Windows, and Sliding Glass Doors?" Who can remind me what that was all about? *Students generally don't have trouble remembering our lesson about Rudine Sims Bishop's (1990) work, as I try to introduce it only a few days before this reading. In fact, it often comes up organically when students are answering the preceding prompt.* How might that concept apply to this moment? *Students often mention how girls might read this section differently than boys. We talk about how readers who have witnessed and dealt with unexpected pregnancies might read the section, as well as people who have experienced either the adoption or foster care systems. They also mention how Benway might be using what she saw in high school to inspire Grace's story.*
4. Grace describes being made to feel like a "sideshow freak" at school since she became pregnant. None of her classmates want to go near her. What might this say about her school's overall culture? *Students tend to assume that her school is probably full of "rich snobs." Or that she goes to a small school where everyone*

has been there forever and has formed lasting, and mean, cliques. I ask students to justify their reasoning. They always have interesting assumptions about class and race for us to collectively tease out.

5. With the answer to the last question in mind, how do you think students in our school would react to Grace's pregnancy? Why? *I often don't have to directly ask this, because it comes up naturally when students engage the last prompt. But when I do, the students tend to have very interesting things to say about both our school's demographics and the culture that the adults in the building model. Students also describe similar instances that their friends have gone through in other schools. Then, they make assertions about why students in those school communities reacted to pregnancies that way.*

The Odyssey

By Homer

Book 9, lines 105–115 (pp. 178–179 in Homer, 1863)

The Context

Grade Level and Discipline: Secondary ELA

The Unit's Goals: Students will better understand how various cultural norms and beliefs are represented in different cultures' storytelling across time.

At This Point in the Text: Odysseus, the hero of the Greek epic poem, is telling his Phaeacian hosts the story about his journey home from the Trojan war. He shares how he raided various settlements, saying, "There I sacked the city, killed the men, but as for the wives and plunder, that rich haul we dragged away from the place—we shared it round so no one, not on my account, would go deprived of his fair share of spoils" (Homer, 1996, p. 212). He then shares about one of these raiding missions that went awry: his men staying too long after a conquest, getting drunk, which allowed his victims to regroup and slaughter many of Odysseus's men. He also tells of the Lotus-eaters, who try to distract his men with fruit that makes them forget their journey home. Finally, he gets to the famous clash with the Cyclops, which he spends the rest of the section describing. This excerpt is his very first description of the Cyclops' land and culture.

The Excerpt

Thence onwards kept we sailing, sad at heart :
And reached the land of the Cyclops ; huge of stature
And ignorant of all fixed laws are they ;
And fully trusting in the deathless gods
They never take in hand to plant a tree
Or plough their land : but without seed or tillage
Grow freely all such plants as these,—wheat, barley,
And fruitful vines that yield abundantly
Wine from their heavy grapes, and showers from Zeus

Give them large increase. No established laws
Nor state-assemblies have they ; but they dwell
In hollow caves among high mountain-peaks :
And each to 'his wives and children lays down law
Of his own will : nor care they one for other.

What Would You Ask Your Students?

____
____
____
____
____
____
____
____
____

What Do I Usually Ask My Students?

1. During Odysseus's journey home, he is committing what we might now call war crimes. Do you think that this character is designed to be a hero or an anti-hero? If he's meant to come off as a hero, what might that say about the culture that produced these stories? How about if he is an anti-hero? *Students have been taught both terms. I will also normally read aloud the section that describes Odysseus's sacking of various cities. Students tend to notice that women were among the plunder that Odysseus "took"—many miss this point when reading for themselves. We don't get too graphic, but we do mention that these women probably faced a horrible fate. Students tend to argue that Odysseus is meant to be a hero to people hearing his story in the Greek Dark Ages, mostly because the bard who tells his story rarely criticizes his behavior. Students also say that this Greek society was probably war-like and valued violence.*
2. Odysseus openly told the Phaeacians about multiple acts of brutality that he committed on the way back from Troy. But

when he speaks about the Cyclops, he calls *them* brutes! Can anyone explain the disconnect between Odysseus's savagery and the way he criticizes the Cyclops? *When students share, they normally describe cognitive dissonance—a phrase they don't tend to know that I introduce as they describe it.* How might we see similar disconnected thinking in today's world? *Without much prompting, kids tend to share various historical and contemporary examples, from slaveholders writing "All men are created equal" in America's founding documents to modern issues with crooked judges and police officers upholding the law.*

3. What are some of the specific reasons that Odysseus gives for the Cyclops being "brutes"? *Kids share any of the following: "They trust the Gods." "The Gods take care of them." "They don't plant crops." "They don't have meeting places." "They don't have laws." "They live as isolated families."* Because of these things, Odysseus seems to think that it's OK to steal from the Cyclops. Have we seen this kind of thinking in history? *Students share historical examples of people using cultural differences to justify oppression.*
4. When the Cyclops later kills some of Odysseus's men, it's written as if he was the bad guy. Is he? *Students tend to debate the proportionality of the Cyclops' response. Odysseus's men stole food, but should they have been killed for it?*
5. Many of the reasons Odysseus has been delayed seem to be his—and his men's—fault. It seems like the audience is supposed to feel sorry for him for not getting home very quickly. At this point in the story, as a reader, are you rooting for him to get home? *This is not the biggest question, but it's important to give kids a chance to respond to a more personal and less academic question. Many kids at this point no longer want to see Odysseus return, while others are still invested despite his awful behavior in this scene and others. It's fun to talk about why.*

Fences

By August Wilson
Act One, Scene Three

The Context

Grade Level and Discipline: Secondary ELA

The Unit's Goals: Students will wrestle with how people determine what they deserve and how authors engage this theme in various kinds of storytelling.

At This Point in the Text: Troy Maxon is a former baseball player who was denied the opportunity to play in the Major Leagues because he was Black. He has carried a lot of anger and frustration about this for years. (One of Troy's habits in the play is speaking in baseball metaphors, as you see in his "crookeds with the straights" phrase at the beginning of the excerpt.) Cory is Troy's teenage son, and he wants to play football. But he must take breaks from his job at the A&P grocery store to go to practice. This angers Troy, who spends the first part of this scene telling Cory how impractical it is to give up a steady job to participate in sports. This excerpt occurs right after the argument has concluded.

The Excerpt

> Troy: You go on down there to that A&P and see if you can get your job back. If you can't do both… then you quit the football team. You've got to take the crooked with the straights.
>
> Cory: Yessir.
>
> (Pause.)
>
> Can I ask you a question?
>
> Troy: What the hell you wanna ask me? Mr. Stawicki [Cory's boss] the one you got the questions for.
>
> Cory: How come you ain't never liked me?
>
> Troy: Liked you? Who the hell say I got to like you? What law is there say I got to like you? Wanna stand up in my face and ask a damn fool a question like that. Talking about liking somebody. Come here, boy, when

I talk to you... Straighten up dammit! I asked you a question... what law is there say I got to like you?

Cory: None.

Troy: Well, all right then! Don't you eat every day? (Pause.) Answer me when I talk to you! Don't you eat every day?

Cory: Yeah.

Troy: N—, as long as you in my house, you put that sir on the end of it when you talk to me!

Cory: Yes... sir.

Troy: You eat every day.

Cory: Yessir!

Troy: Got clothes on your back.

Cory: Yessir.

Troy: Why you think that is?

Cory: Cause of you.

Troy: Aw, hell I know it's cause of me... but why do you think that is?

Cory (Hesitant.): Cause you like me.

Troy: Like you? I go out of here every morning... bust my butt putting up with them crackers every day... cause I like you? You about the biggest fool I ever saw.

(Pause.)

It's my job, it's my responsibility! You understand that? A man got to take care of his family. You live in my house, sleep on my bedclothes, fill your belly up on my food... cause you my son. You my flesh and blood. Not cause I like you! Cause it's my duty to take care of you. I owe a responsibility to you!

Let's get this straight here, before it go along any further... I ain't got to like you. Mr. Rand don't give me my money come payday 'cause he likes me. He gives me cause he owe me. I done given you everything I had to give you. I gave you your life! Me and your mama worked that out between us. And liking your black ass wasn't part of the bargain. Don't you try and go through life worrying about if somebody like you or not. You best be making sure they doing right by you. You understand what I'm saying, boy?

Cory: Yessir.

Troy: Then get the hell out of my face, and get on down to that A&P.

What Would You Ask Your Students?

What Do I Usually Ask My Students?

1. Why do you think the football argument ends with Cory asking why Troy has never liked him? Does he genuinely think his dad doesn't like him? *Students: "Cory notices that his dad doesn't value his happiness. If he did, he would be more reasonable about the job and football." Most tend to take his question as genuine. Some students, however, think that Cory might be trying to guilt his father into changing his mind.*
2. *We watch the above scene acted out in the 2016* Fences *movie, followed by the 2010* Fences *Broadway play. Both clips can be found on YouTube. Denzel Washington plays Troy in both.* What did we notice about the audience's reaction in the Broadway version? *Students: "There was a lot of laughter!"* Did this surprise you? *Some students are always surprised, while others are not. Some even share how uncomfortable they were watching the Broadway version because the live audiences' reaction was drastically different from their own.* Why do you think the audience reacted like this? *Some students argue that there was something different about Denzel's performance. Some talk about the difference between the controlled camera shots in a film and seeing a play on stage. I push them to justify how the differences may influence the audience's reaction. Some students say that the laughter was due to their discomfort. Again, I ask them to justify why this might be so. Importantly, students tend to mention how many in*

the audience may be remembering similar conversations with their parents. The laugh, then, may have been a shared cultural moment.

3. Do you think that Troy is in the right or in the wrong here? Why or why not? *This usually sparks a good debate. Students weigh the merit of Troy's argument. On one side, Cory shouldn't concern himself with whether people in power like him. On the other, isn't it Troy's responsibility to be a loving parent? Students bring up all sorts of things, most interestingly unpacking masculinity and how in many cultures, fathers are often less affectionate than mothers, and how this might affect children.*
4. Troy lists a series of his responsibilities. He does not see liking his children as one of his responsibilities as a father. Do you agree or disagree with him? Why? *The responses vary. Students tend to debate whether there is a difference between liking one's children and loving them. This can be one of those more emotionally tough questions for kids to engage, especially if they were wronged by a parent or family member and feel like they deserve better.*

Born a Crime

By Trevor Noah
Chapter 15, pages 194–195

The Context

Grade Level and Discipline: Secondary humanities

The Unit's Goals: Students will better understand how our cultures influence our identities. They will also understand cultural relativism in memoirs and other forms of literature.

At This Point in the Text: The comedian Trevor Noah describes an emotionally and culturally complex incident from his teenage years, where he and a group of friends were hired to perform at a Jewish school in South Africa. Noah's friend is a great dancer, and his name happens to be Hitler. The hosts, understandably, are hurt and offended by the boys chanting "Go Hitler!" as the boy dances. A teacher from the school and Noah get into a shouting match, neither one of them fully understanding why the other is so upset. In the following excerpt, Noah explains to readers why the name Hitler is rare but not unheard of in South Africa.

The Excerpt

> Westerners are shocked and confused by [the habit of naming children "Hitler"], but really it's a case of the West reaping what it has sown. The colonial powers carved up Africa, put the black man to work, and did not properly educate him. White people don't talk to black people. So why would black people know what's going on in the white man's world? Because of that, many black people in South Africa don't really know who Hitler was. My own grandfather thought "a hitler" was a kind of army tank that was helping the Germans win the war. Because that's what he took from what he heard on the news. For many black South Africans, the story of the war was that there was someone called Hitler and he was the reason the Allies were losing the war. This Hitler was so powerful that at some point black people had to go help white people fight against him—and if the white man has to stoop to ask the black man for help fighting someone, that someone must be the toughest guy of all time. So if you want your dog to be tough, you name your dog Hitler. If you want your kid to be tough, you name your kid Hitler. There's a good chance you've got an uncle named Hitler. It's just a thing.

There is also this to consider: The name Hitler does not offend a black South African because Hitler is not the worst thing a black South African can imagine. Every country thinks their history is the most important, and that's especially true in the West. But if black South Africans could go back in time and kill one person, Cecil Rhodes would come up before Hitler. If people in the Congo could go back in time and kill one person, Belgium's King Leopold would come way before Hitler. If Native Americans could go back in time and kill one person, it would probably be Christopher Columbus or Andrew Jackson.

What Would You Ask Your Students?

____

____

____

____

____

____

____

____

____

What Do I Usually Ask My Students?

1. Nobody in the West names their children Hitler. Why? *Students share obvious answers about the Holocaust.* Numbers vary, but this even affects the name "Adolf," which used to be relatively popular before World War II and is now super rare. *I quickly share with students just how rare the name is.*
2. Noah explains why this naming trend is different in South Africa. Can anybody describe this difference in their own words? *Students share. But if they have trouble with the prompt, I ask as many of the following follow-up prompts as necessary, while referring to the excerpt's second paragraph as a source.*
   - What did apartheid do to Black people and White people? *"Keep them apart."*
   - Would this have included schools? *"Yes."*
   - So many South African Black kids would not have much access to information about European history. And they also

would not know anyone who has experienced the Holocaust, so they wouldn't learn about it that way, either, right?

- What does Noah say that the average Black South African would know about Hitler? *"That he was winning the war for a while, and this made Europeans scared."*
- How scared were they? *"So scared that White people asked Black people for help!"*
- Why would this have been a big deal to Black South Africans? *"Black South Africans see White people going to great lengths to stay separate from them. For Whites to ask Blacks for help via desegregation would then be a huge deal."*
- So in the West, "Hitler" means "Holocaust." What does Noah say it means to an average Black South African? *"Power" and so on.*

3. Is there a possibility that the South African educational system might have deliberately taught Black South Africans about the Holocaust in an inadequate way? If so, why? Do we see any other times when folks in power might limit what is taught to specific groups of young people?
4. Noah then talks about why some Black South Africans are not instinctively offended by the name Hitler, even after learning about his brutality. What do you think about Noah's argument (in a paragraph not shown in this limited excerpt) that "every country thinks their history is the most important, and that's especially true in the West"? *Students tend to agree.* Can anyone think of examples to back this up? *Students often share that when they were younger, they were surprised to learn that holidays like Thanksgiving and July 4 are only for Americans. They also often share that they don't know much about the history of other countries.*
5. Noah alludes to the popular "Would you go back in time and kill baby Hitler?" moral dilemma, but he argues that a South African would substitute Cecil Rhodes for Hitler, while a Congolese person would sub in King Leopold. As famous as Hitler's atrocities are, Noah argues that neither group of Africans

would think he's important enough to be the example of utmost cruelty. Why?

6. How many of you know who Cecil Rhodes is? How about King Leopold? *There are almost never any raised hands. I briefly tell students about both figures' brutality.* Should you be blamed for not knowing these names? *Students: "No! Nobody taught us!"* How might it be harmful to not know about historical atrocities from around the globe? How might it be harmful to not know about current atrocities?
7. In the section immediately after this excerpt, Noah argues that the reason that the Holocaust is seen as the preeminent atrocity in modern human history is that Hitler and the Nazis kept records—while *other* awful people and governments did not. What do you think about this thesis? Can you think of any examples that would either back up or undermine his argument? *Students share. The richness of this response generally depends on whether students in the class can reference atrocities other than American antebellum slavery, which they all know about, and South African apartheid, which* Born a Crime *is highlighting. Generally, students tend to agree that having casualty numbers is better than not having them. But they also share that seeing or reading compelling human stories, like* The Diary of Anne Frank, *also helps people care more about an atrocity, regardless of where it took place.*
8. Noah chose to offer this explanation of why South Africans sometimes name kids Hitler—it's essentially an analytical essay—before telling his story about the dance party at the Jewish school. As a writer, he didn't have to do that. Why do you think he ordered this chapter this way? *Students tend to say that his explanation helps the audience to make sense of the following dance scene.* How does Noah's essay influence the humor of the following story? *Students share opinions. Answers can also rigorously engage various theories about humor, if these theories have been taught. I tend to ask students if Noah's story is able to achieve what the Humor Research Lab (n.d.) calls a "benign violation."*

The Milgram Experiment

The Context

Grade Level and Discipline: Secondary humanities, psychology, or statistics

The Unit's Goals: Students will understand how social experiments are structured and what we can learn from them.

The Background: This video (Madarabalhazred, 2016) is a reproduction of Stanley Milgram's famous 1961 social experiment that aired on a BBC show *Horizon* in its 2008–2009 season. In the video, volunteer participants are divided into two groups: "teachers" and "learners." The teachers are tasked with asking memory questions to the learners. When the learners eventually get questions wrong, the teachers are told by the "scientist" to administer a painful electric shock. With each wrong answer, the voltage of the shock increases. The learner screams in pain and asks to be let out. Eventually, the shocks reach a dangerous, then a deadly level. By then, the learner has gone silent. What the teacher doesn't know is that the learner is an actor, and they have not been receiving any shocks. (The screams are playing from a prerecorded tape.) The study is not about memory at all but about obedience. Milgram wants to know if the teacher will call a stop to the experiment, despite the scientist—who is also an actor—urging them to continue.

The Video: www.dailymotion.com/video/x4xk2sy

What Would You Ask Your Students?

What Do I Usually Ask My Students?

1. What parts of the experiment seem purposefully designed? *I often ask this prompt right before students start watching the video. I then pause the video right after the participants have been assigned their roles, pointing out that the teacher thought that he or she was assigned this role randomly. This, of course, means that the teacher should know that, if the tables were turned, they could have been the one receiving the shocks. If I feel like students need more modeling, I point out that this teacher then received a sample shock from the device. This reinforces their belief that the shocks are real. After getting these examples, students tend to not have much trouble pointing out other elements of the experiment's design that seem important.*
2. Which one of these design elements do you think might have been the most important, and why? What would change if this design element was modified or taken away? *A common answer is that the teacher could not see the learner being electrocuted. Students think that the results would be different if the teacher could actually see an actor pretending to be electrocuted. This regularly sparks an interesting debate about whether—and why—visual stimuli of violence are more gut-wrenching than the auditory stimuli of someone screaming.*
3. *I pause the video right before it reveals just how many teachers end up delivering a lethal 450-volt shock.* So, how many, out of 12, do you think went all the way? Why?
4. *The numbers are revealed in the video: 9 out of 12 participants went all the way to a lethal voltage in this re-creation, and over 65 percent did in the original Milgram experiment.* So what do you think? *Students are nearly always floored.*
5. What do you think of the 19-year-old student? She is smiling throughout the experiment, even chuckling when she asks, "Have we killed him?"
    - What do you think explains her facial reactions? *Students: "She's a sociopath!" Other students: "She's just overwhelmed."*
    - The researcher argues that she is "the classic example of what Milgram shows, that somebody who, at face value, poses

no threat to anybody, can at these kinds of circumstances, proceed to the point of inflicting severe levels of pain." Why might this realization be important? *Students say that they should always be careful with others. Others point out that this might not be the best way to live. There are often good exchanges about this.*

6. The researcher in the video uses the term "diffusion of responsibility" to explain the participants' continuing to up the voltage despite their peers' screaming. He argues that the teachers do not find themselves responsible for the damage that they are causing, because science has made them do it. What do you think about this? Is the researcher right? If not, how else do you explain the teacher's behavior? If yes, where do you see other examples of people diffusing their own responsibility for doing bad things? *Students talk about issues like factory farming, the exploitive labor used in fast fashion, and so on. They say that we tend to say other people are ultimately responsible.*
7. *I point out that one of the teachers had slumped down in what looks like despair at the end of the experiment.* Should we be allowed to use human subjects for experiments like this? Why or why not? What ground rules should govern experiments that use real people?

The Ethics of Engineering

Based on an interview with John Kamal, Philadelphia engineering teacher

The Context

Grade Level and Discipline: Sophomore engineering

The Unit's Goals: For students to explore their ethical selves and to think deeply about how their sense of ethics applies to their work in the engineering program and their potential lives as professional engineers.

The Background: This is the first day of the engineering elective, and the discussion generally lasts three days.

The Quote: "Ethics is about acting in a way that is consistent with your own moral code—your knowing right from wrong."

What Would You Ask Your Students?

What Does John Usually Ask His Students?

1. What do I personally base my ethics and moral code on? *Students share about their religious backgrounds and lessons from their parents. Some say that they've thought about ethics deeply and have come up with their own moral code.*
2. Why do you think I am talking about this in engineering class? Why might ethics be important in the field of engineering?

Students tend to talk about how, if engineers make an unethical error, it could hurt or even kill somebody.

3. How might unethical behavior from an engineer have different results than a lawyer or a doctor? *Students, after a while, share that if a doctor behaves unethically, they could kill somebody. If a lawyer behaves unethically, they might send somebody to prison. But if an engineer behaves unethically, they could kill 500 people! These victims might be on a plane, or a bridge, and so on.*
4. Is it ethical to take $1,000 from a client to fudge the results of your analysis of their new product? How about $100,000? *Students tend to agree that for $1,000, it's unethical. The fun exchanges start when the number gets higher, as students find uses for the money. Eventually, John likes to ask holdouts, "What's your number?"*
5. Is it ethical to approve a product design that has a small chance of being unsafe? *Initially, the general answer is no! John then asks students, "Do you drive in a car? Doesn't a car have a chance of being unsafe?" Students wrestle with what amount of risk is tolerable, knowing that getting to 0 percent is impossible. John often asks, "Who gets to decide the threshold of acceptable risk?"*
6. Is it ethical to help a client optimize their business for profitability? How about if that means you will hurt the environment? *Most students are OK with an engineer helping a business be more profitable. Some students express anti-capitalist sentiments. John nudges these kids to consider the smartphones in their hands, which have heavy metals in them that can't be perfectly disposed of. He similarly will point to their water bottles that were just shipped across the country. Doesn't that hurt the environment? Where is the line and, again, who defines where it is?*
7. Is it ethical to exaggerate the importance of your work to help your career? *Conversation goes similarly to earlier prompts in the conversation.*
8. *John adds other ethical dilemmas from his career as an engineer. Conversation goes similarly to earlier prompts in the conversation.*

9. There is this idea around ethics called "the red-face rule." Basically, it means that if you (an engineer) were at a party, and someone told someone that you care about (your spouse, your child, etc.) something that you did, would you feel ashamed? What do you think of this rule?

Key Quote from Interview

"I want them to think more deeply about things that they know... and things that they don't know yet."

A Calculus Inquiry: The Box Problem

Based on an interview with Brad Latimer, Philadelphia mathematics teacher

The Context

Grade Level and Discipline: Calculus

The Unit's Goals: Students will be able to apply derivative shortcuts to solve a variety of problems.

The Background: This is mid-year, after students have learned all of the derivative shortcut rules. This is an introduction to how to use these rules to solve more advanced problems.

The Task: In your group, you are going to make an open-topped box by cutting a square out of each corner of rectangular cardboard, all the same size, then folding up the flaps to form the box, as illustrated below.

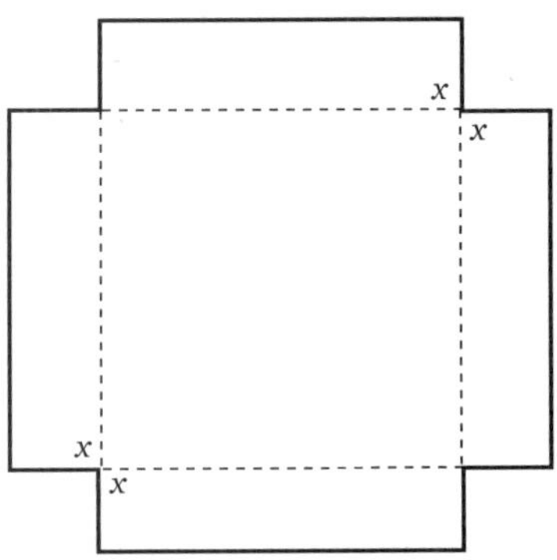

Your challenge: You and one other group will receive the same size piece of cardboard. Your goal is to figure out how to make the cut-out squares in order to maximize the volume of the box, and then create your box. Don't forget to write down the exact dimensions of your box and calculate the volume. Whichever group creates a box with a larger volume wins.

What Would You Ask Your Students?

What Does Brad Usually Ask His Students?

With this task and discussion, Brad leans completely into student-centered inquiry. This means that a lot of the prompting is Brad answering student questions with his own questions. Here are the common student questions, and how he responds with prompts.

1. Students: What equation are we working with?
   Brad: Well, what do we want? *Students say, "The largest box," "The volume," "Dimensions to maximize volume," and so on.*
2. Students: I know the equation for volume, but I don't know how to work with this. There are too many variables.
   Brad: OK, is there a way that your group can work with *other* variables? *Students say, "I guess we need to find a way to get rid of variables, or we use different variables."*
3. Students: How do I know that I have the right answer?
   Brad: "What do you think?" *Students say, "I could plug into the equation," or "I could look at a graph," or "I could examine a table of values."*

At the same time, students are trying to figure out the problem in small groups. These are some of the questions that they ask each other.

1. Why wouldn't we just make the cuts really little? Wouldn't that maximize the base? *Somone else will respond that if they do that, they'd be multiplying length, width, and height, and the height would be very small.*

2. OK, why wouldn't we just make the cuts really big? *Someone else will respond that the height would be really big, but the length and width would be very small.*
3. Can we make a table of values? *Someone else would wonder how to most accurately set up the table. For example, do they only consider whole numbers? If they consider decimals, how many decimal places do they round to?*

At the end of the period, the students try to physically make the box. (As it comes down to small decimal points, the kids just do their best to get as close as possible.) Brad then does a big reveal of the right answer, and the group nearest to it wins. The next day, he asks one of the groups that won to come before the class and explain their logic. There are always some groups that have come close to the right answer using other methods— and some who actually figured out the "Calculus method" of solving the problem, and therefore have the exact answer. He picks these Calculus method groups to present. He asks these groups questions throughout their presentation to make their reasoning clear to their classmates.

Key Quote from Interview

"This activity and discussion takes *a while*! But it's one of those deals where I could show them how do this problem in 15 minutes… or I can spend a full class period where they are wrestling with it, and they really internalize it. Every kid at the end of the year remembers doing this. So I'll opt for that 10 times out of 10."

The Characteristics of Life

Based on an interview with Steph Sessa, Philadelphia biochemistry teacher

The Context

Grade Level and Discipline: 9th grade biochemistry

The Unit's Goals: Students will be able to describe the characteristics of life shared by all prokaryotic and eukaryotic organisms.

The Background: This conversation is held after teaching about protein synthesis. Students have looked at DNA and how it makes us who we are. Then the class zooms out to look at cells. After this unit, the class will move into body systems and dissections.

The Seven Basic Characteristics of Life:

1. Made of cells
2. Need and use energy (metabolism)
3. Respond to stimuli and changes in the environment
4. Keep a balance (homeostasis)
5. Grow and develop
6. Reproduce and pass down genes
7. Adapt through evolution

What Would You Ask Your Students?

What Does Steph Normally Ask Her Students?

1. What does it mean to be living? *Students tend to struggle with this. Usually because the class has just focused on DNA, they say, "Has DNA." They'll say that a living thing has to grow. They'll get a few of the characteristics, but rarely all.*
2. What do all living things have in common? *Students often say, "Movement." This leads to conversations about how plants move. They'll say that living things grow and so on.*
3. Is fire alive? Are icicles alive? Why or why not? *These prompts trip students up. Students innately know that these things aren't alive, but they have trouble articulating why. They'll say, "Fire doesn't reproduce" or "Icicles don't grow." Steph will ask, "If an ember moves to create another fire, is that not reproducing?" And with the icicles, Steph will say "Don't icicles grow from baby icicles to big icicles?" Eventually, students will bring up DNA, cells, or evolution.*
4. There are seven "characteristics of life" that biologists uniformly agree upon. What do you think they are? *Students tend to get some of them. They tend not to get "responds to stimuli" and "adapts through evolution." Steph will bring up scenarios related to the earlier prompts, such as, "Have you ever noticed that a plant will move toward sunlight? That is responding to stimuli."*
5. What characteristics of life does fire not have? How about icicles? *Students will say that the wood has cells, but the fire itself does not.*

Key Quote from Interview

"I actually don't like cells as a unit, because [kids] can't see them. Right? They have to see them under a microscope—which is cool—but there's not a lot of immediate context for themselves. Like, why should kids care? But by relating cells back to the big question, 'What is life?' . . . the prompts can hook many more students. Students think, 'Hey, a cell is a characteristic that makes us who we are, makes us alive.' And plus, this way connects the unit to our school's identity theme. We can talk about *who we are* through the characteristics of life. And then it's a lot more relatable to students."

Supervised Injection Sites

Based on an interview with Brian Kelly, Philadelphia health and physical education teacher

The Context

Grade Level and Discipline: 10th grade health

The Unit's Goals: Cover the seven types and categories of drugs, as well as the effects that they have on humans. Students learn how drug use affects the local environment, which for these students is Philadelphia, Pennsylvania.

The Background: Brian tries to link each type of drug with a local crisis that it has caused. Before this conversation, students have already discussed the opioid crisis. They have discussed the role of Big Pharma and watched clips from the TV show *Dopesick*.

The Resources:

- The episode "Philly Dope" from the show *Drugs, Inc* (2013): www.youtube.com/watch?v=nR7V4G1eHPE
- Pro supervised injection site article (Finke & Chan, 2022): www.aafp.org/pubs/afp/issues/2022/0500/p454.pdf
- Anti supervised injection site article (Rosen, 2020): www.justice.gov/archives/opa/blog/philadelphia-inquirer-op-ed-safe-injection-sites-enable-drug-users-and-endanger-communities

What Would You Ask Your Students?

What Does Brian Normally Ask His Students?

1. Do you know where Kensington is? Have you seen it? *Some students have, and they have to travel through the neighborhood on the way to school.*
2. What do you see there? *Students: "A lot of drug addicts."* What else do you see? *Students: "A lot of cops, but you still see a lot of drug activity."*
3. We know that Kensington is one of the largest open-air drug markets in the entire world. Whose fault is that? *Some students say that it's addicts' fault. Some say that it's the cops' fault. Some say that it's the politicians' fault. With each one, Brian asks students to justify their answer.*
4. What would you do about the situation if you lived in Kensington? *Some students: "I would never live there."* There are people who actually have to live there. Is it fair to them to have to see all of that every day? *Some students: "They should move."* That's not as easy as it might seem, though, right? *Students discuss some of the circumstances that would keep a family from being able to move.*
5. One at least partial solution might be supervised injection sites. After reading the articles, who is for supervised injection sites in Kensington? Who is against them? *Students raise their hands for either one.*

6. For those who raised their hands in support of supervised injection sites, would you support one down the street from your house? *Some students say, "Oh! I thought you meant in Kensington!"* No, what if it was down the street from your house, wherever you live *now*? *This causes some students to admit that it changes their level of support. Other students hold fast, saying that the goal is to get people a safer environment, where if they overdose, there is a nurse there. Or if they need a clean needle, it's there. Also, there are resources to start getting clean if they are ready.* Why did many of your opinions change depending on how close the injection site was to your house?
7. For those who are totally against supervised injection sites, wouldn't you want a loved one who was addicted to drugs to have a safer environment? *Students' answers vary. Some emphatically say yes. Most often there are more guarded answers like, "I don't know. Maybe. If they were close to me, probably."*

Key Quote from Interview

"I try to get them to think. It's easy to come up with an answer right away—based on how they live now—but they always have to put themselves in other situations. The answer that they give me now, is that the answer that they would stick with if [their lived experience] changed? And, true, a lot of times, kids pretty much stick with what their original answer was, but when I throw that devil's advocate question at them, it puts them in the shoes of someone who is actually going through the situation *right now.* A lot of times our kids don't think like that, and that's OK, because they're kids. But it's our job to push them."

A Quick Departmental PD Idea

I hope that you have found this section useful. Before leaving it, I want to make a suggestion for professional development: Teachers within any department can basically do what I did here, starting with pulling a favorite passage from a curricular text.

Then, after sharing the passage's basic context and any relevant curricular goals, they could ask one another what prompts they would ask students about this passage. Then, after a few minutes to draft some questions, teachers could reveal—and then discuss—the prompts they actually ask students. For an added layer of perspective, teachers might even invite trusted students into the conversation.

Conclusion: Jumping Up on Tables

I'll always remember a conversation I had with my principal after a mandatory classroom observation. It was midway through my first year, and I was starting to experience some consistent successes in the classroom for the first time. My students seemed to like me, and they seemed to be enjoying my class. I was charismatic, funny, and caring, and I had the boundless energy that 22-year-old teachers are known for. I can't recall what lesson was being observed, but it featured a class discussion, and I had *rocked* it.

My principal started off our reflection by saying as much, an encouraging habit that I've never taken for granted. So many teachers throughout the country have come to associate mandatory observations with checklists, nitpicking, and grandstanding. The appearance of an administrator at our classroom door makes our hearts beat wildly, as we grip dry-erase markers in damping palms, hoping we'd remembered to post the objective on the board. We worry about administrators focusing on the one student with her head down or sidling up to the student who never pays attention to ask him about our lesson. I experienced all of this at my first school, and I was happy to discover my then (and current) principal's far more generous approach to observations. He told me what I was doing well, and I felt pretty good about myself.

Then, crucially, he added a caveat that I have never forgotten. In the discussion that I had just led, I had expended *a lot* of energy. It was the kind of "Rip it out!" performance made famous by the fictional

Mr. Keating in *Dead Poets Society*. Inspirational stuff. Yet Robin Williams's famous character only had to maintain that jumping-on-tables theatricality through a couple classroom scenes and a montage. I had to do it for a career. My principal knew that, as a classroom lifer, my race was going to be more a marathon than a sprint. And when I was older, when I had kids of my own, when I eventually took on other responsibilities in my life, I would not consistently have "Rip it out!" energy. Sure, this kind of vigor would come in bursts, as this or that conversation excited me. But he told me that day-in, day-out success would depend on whether I developed a system for my conversations. One that didn't rely as much on personal showmanship.

This stuck with me for many reasons. Mostly, it brought my mom to mind, who, while battling health problems that affected her mobility, taught mostly from a chair in the front of her classroom. Throughout my entire childhood, I remember adults coming up to us on the street to say, "Hi, Mrs. Kay! It's me, [insert name]! You were such a good teacher!" Her lessons were memorable because they were imaginative, well-planned, and thoughtfully executed. Not because she jumped up on tables. My principal was essentially saying, "If you want to make it to almost 40 years, be more like your mom." There is nothing I wanted more, then or now. And to get there, I would need to learn how to craft discussion prompts that did the heavy lifting for me.

In this short book, I have tried to show the system I've discovered in the two decades since that memorable observation. I hope that after reading Part I, you have found ways to write discussion prompts that spark deep exchanges between students, without feeling like you always need to be on stage. I hope that the exercises in Part II have given both new and veteran teachers a chance to practice writing prompts without the pressure of a looming class period. As I argued in the Introduction, the hard work of crafting powerful discussion prompts may end up being the most important part of our pedagogy in the AI age. Ultimately, we are in a position to help young humans learn how to discuss big issues with other humans, to communicate honestly, and to listen. To be prepared for the many hard conversations that await them as the world keeps on changing.

It is an important task, but it's one that I am confident we are up to.

Acknowledgments

I'd like to thank my wife, Cait, for providing honest, insightful, and comprehensive feedback on every draft of this book; my father, Rosamond, for the decades of mind-sharpening conversation that model the discourse I want for my students; and my aunt, Connie, for her unconditional love and support. I also thank my father-in-law, David, for taking such great care of our family.

Thanks to my principal and great friend, Chris Lehmann, for all the professional opportunities that led to the writing of this book. I similarly thank my colleagues who generously agreed to be interviewed: Brad Latimer, Steph Sessa, John Kamal, and Brian Kelly.

Much love to the generations of SLA students who have made teaching them the best job in the world.

I will always be grateful to my content editor, Bill Varner, for his patience, expertise, and encouragement. (We finally did a book together all the way through!) And much appreciation to my production editor, Liz Wegner, for making sure the final product was as polished and well organized as possible.

Finally, thank you, Dia and Benni. Daddy loves you.

References

bana hayat Ver. (2014, October 23). *The allegory of the long spoons* [Video]. YouTube. https://www.youtube.com/watch?v=e4lI8e33U2A&t=1s

Bats, J. (2022, January 31). *8 effective strategies of retaining fitness clients after the January gym rush.* ContentBASE. https://contentbase.com/blog/january-gym-rush-retention/

Belluck, P. (2001, May 7). Nuns offer clues to Alzheimer's and aging. *New York Times.* https://www.nytimes.com/2001/05/07/us/nuns-offer-clues-to-alzheimer-s-and-aging.html

Benway, R. (2017). *Far from the tree.* HarperCollins.

Bishop, R. S. (1990). Mirrors, windows, and sliding glass doors. *Perspectives: Choosing and Using Books for the Classroom, 6*(3).

Bregman, R. (2020, May 9). The real Lord of the Flies: What happened when six boys were shipwrecked for 15 months. *The Guardian.* https://www.theguardian.com/books/2020/may/09/the-real-lord-of-the-flies-what-happened-when-six-boys-were-shipwrecked-for-15-months

Bullhead Entertainment. (2008, April 19). *The cave: An adaptation of Plato's allegory in clay* [Video]. YouTube. https://www.youtube.com/watch?v=69F7GhASOdM&t=1s

Cisneros, S. (1991). Eleven. In *Woman hollering creek and other stories* (pp. 6–9). Vintage Books.

Connor, L. (2019, November 23). 6 New Years resolution gym statistics you need to know. *Glofox.* https://www.glofox.com/blog/6-new-years-resolution-gym-statistics-you-need-to-know/

Daniels, H., & Zemelman, S. (2004). *Subjects matter: Every teacher's guide to content-area reading.* Heinemann.

de Bruin, N. (2021, December 3). What is the January gym rush—and why should you care? *Virtuagym.* https://business.virtuagym.com/blog/what-is-the-january-gym-rush-and-why-should-you-care

Dobbs v. Jackson Women's Health Organization (U.S. Supreme Court June 24, 2022). https://www.supremecourt.gov/opinions/21pdf/19-1392_6j37.pdf

Drugs, Inc. (2013, September 29). *Philly dope* [Video]. YouTube. https://www.youtube.com/watch?v=nR7V4G1eHPE

Dure, B. (2015, September 24). Winning isn't everything; it's the only thing. Right? *The Guardian.* https://www.theguardian.com/sport/2015/sep/24/winning-everything-sports

FencesBroadway. (2010, May 3). *Fences clip: How come you ain't never liked me?* [Video]. YouTube. https://www.youtube.com/watch?v=UBTXS42dj40

Finke, J., & Chan, J. (2022). The case for supervised injection sites in the United States. *American Family Physician, 105*(5), 444–445. https://www.aafp.org/pubs/afp/issues/2022/0500/p454.pdf

Gewertz, C. (2018, August 15). What do employers want in a new hire? Mostly, good speaking skills. *Education Week*. https://www.edweek.org/teaching-learning/what-do-employers-want-in-a-new-hire-mostly-good-speaking-skills/2018/08

Gladwell, M. (2019). *Talking to strangers*. Little, Brown.

Golding, W. (1954). *Lord of the flies*. Faber & Faber.

Grann, D. (2023). *The Wager: A tale of shipwreck, mutiny, and murder*. Doubleday.

Homer. (1863). *The odyssey* (T. S. Norgate, Trans.). Williams & Norgate.

Homer. (1996). *The odyssey* (R. Fagles, Trans.). Viking.

Humor Research Lab. (n.d.). Benign violation theory. https://humorresearchlab.com/benign-violation-theory/

Im, P. (2017, January 10). *Psychology: The Stanford prison experiment – BBC Documentary* [Video]. YouTube. https://www.youtube.com/watch?v=F4txhN13y6A

Jacobs, T. (2007). Ten Supreme Court cases every teen should know. *New York Times*. https://archive.nytimes.com/www.nytimes.com/learning/teachers/featured_articles/20080915monday.html?...1

Kay, M. R. (2018). *Not light, but fire: How to lead meaningful race conversations*. Routledge.

Kincaid, J. (1978, June 19). Girl. *The New Yorker*. https://www.newyorker.com/magazine/1978/06/26/girl

Madarabalhazred. (2016). *The Milgram experiment repeated* [Video]. https://www.dailymotion.com/video/x4xk2sy

McCormick, P. (2006). *Sold*. Hyperion Paperbacks.

McTighe, J., & Wiggins, G. (2014). Improve curriculum, assessment, and instruction using the Understanding by Design framework. ASCD. https://files.ascd.org/staticfiles/ascd/pdf/siteASCD/publications/ASCD_UBD_whitepaper.pdf

Merriam-Webster. (n.d.). Prompt. In *Merriam-Webster.com dictionary*. Retrieved June 18, 2024, from https://www.merriam-webster.com/dictionary/prompt

Movieclips. (2019, February 22). *Fences (2016)–I ain't got to like you scene* [Video]. YouTube. https://www.youtube.com/watch?v=tVxYCeRXzGo

NFL Films. (2021, February 4). *Vince Lombardi: The coach who put Green Bay on the map | A football life* [Video]. YouTube. https://www.youtube.com/watch?v=njlGLMYopLo

Noah, T. (2016). *Born a crime: Stories from a South African childhood*. Spiegel & Grau.

Obergefell v. Hodges. (U.S. Supreme Court June 26, 2015). https://www.justice.gov/sites/default/files/crt/legacy/2015/06/26/obergefellhodgesopinion.pdf

Ohio House Bill 327. (2021). https://ohiohouse.gov/legislation/134/hb327/committee

Pennsylvania Department of Education. (2014). *Pennsylvania Core Standards English language arts grades 6–12*. https://www.education.pa.gov/Teachers%20-%20Administrators/Curriculum/ELA/Pages/default.aspx

Piaget, J. (1954). *The construction of reality in the child*. Basic Books.

Rosen, J. A. (2020, February 3). *Philadelphia Inquirer* op-ed: Safe injection sites enable drug users and endanger communities. U.S. Department of Justice. https://www.justice.gov/archives/opa/blog/philadelphia-inquirer-op-ed-safe-injection-sites-enable-drug-users-and-endanger-communities

Rosenblatt, L. M. (1994). *The reader, the text, the poem: The transactional theory of the literary work*. Southern Illinois University Press.

Ross, G. (Director). (1998). *Pleasantville* [Film]. New Line Cinema; Larger Than Life Productions.

Schaeffer, K. (2021, November 12). Among many U.S. children, reading for fun has become less common, federal data shows. *Pew Research Center*. https://www.pewresearch.org/short-reads/2021/11/12/among-many-u-s-children-reading-for-fun-has-become-less-common-federal-data-shows/

Shi, D. (Director). (2018). *Bao* [Short film]. Pixar Animation Studios; Walt Disney Pictures.

Silverstein, S. (1964). *The giving tree*. HarperCollins.

SM East Harbinger. (2016, September 27). *Debate: Colin Kaepernick* [Video]. YouTube. https://www.youtube.com/watch?v=WqhgahPB1So

Strong, D. (Executive Producer). (2021). *Dopesick* [TV series]. John Goldwyn Productions; 20th Century Fox Television; 20th Television; Danny Strong Productions; Fox 21 Television Studios; The Littlefield Company; Touchstone Television.

Texas House Bill 3979. (2021). https://capitol.texas.gov/tlodocs/87R/billtext/pdf/HB03979I.pdf

Tinker v. Des Moines. (U.S. Supreme Court, February 24, 1969). https://www.uscourts.gov/educational-resources/educational-activities/facts-and-case-summary-tinker-v-des-moines

Wiggins, G., & McTighe, J. (2005). *Understanding by design* (Expanded 2nd ed.). ASCD.

Wilson, A. (1986). *Fences*. Plume.

Wright, R. (1940). *Native son*. Harper & Brothers.

Wright, R. (1944). *Black boy*. Harper & Brothers.

Zusak, M. (2005). *The book thief*. Alfred A. Knopf.

Zwick, E. (Director). (2008). *Defiance* [Film]. Paramount Vantage; Grosvenor Pictures; Bedford Falls Company; Defiance Productions.

Index

The letter *f* following a page locator denotes a figure.

About the Author

Matthew R. Kay is a proud product of Philadelphia's public schools and a founding teacher at Science Leadership Academy (SLA). He is also the founder and co-director of Philly Slam League, a nonprofit organization that shows young people the power of their voices through weekly spoken word competitions and workshops.

Kay deeply believes in the importance of earnest and mindful class discussions. Furthermore, he believes that any teacher who is willing to put in the hard work of reflection can, through the practice of discrete skills, become a better discussion leader. Driven by these convictions, he is passionate about designing professional development that teachers find valuable. Kay is the author of the bestselling *Not Light, but Fire: How to Lead Meaningful Race Conversations in the Classroom,* as well as the co-author of *We're Gonna Keep on Talking: How to Lead Meaningful Race Conversations in the Elementary Classroom* and *Answers to Your Biggest Questions About Teaching Middle and High School ELA.*

Kay lives in Philadelphia with his wife, Cait, and his daughters, Adia Sherrill and Bennu Jane.

Related Resources: Class Discussions

At the time of publication, the following resources were available (ASCD stock numbers in parentheses).

Amplify Student Voices: Equitable Practices to Build Confidence in the Classroom by AnnMarie Baines, Diana Medina, Caitlin Healy (#122061)

The Best Class You Never Taught: How Spider Web Discussion Can Turn Students into Learning Leaders by Alexis Wiggins (#117017)

Demystifying Discussion: How to Teach and Assess Academic Conversation Skills, K–5 by Jennifer Orr (#122003)

Generating Formative Feedback (Quick Reference Guide) by Jackie Acree Walsh (#QRG122060)

Guiding Meaningful Math Conversations (Quick Reference Guide) by Laney Sammons (#QRG117056)

Improving Classroom Discussion (Quick Reference Guide) by Jackie Acree Walsh (#QRG117053)

Now That's a Good Question! How to Promote Cognitive Rigor Through Classroom Questioning by Erik M. Francis (#116004)

Questioning for Classroom Discussion: Purposeful Speaking, Engaged Listening, Deep Thinking by Jackie Acree Walsh and Beth Dankert Sattes (#115012)

Questioning for Formative Feedback: Meaningful Dialogue to Improve Learning by Jackie Acree Walsh (#119006)

Students Taking Action Together: 5 Teaching Techniques to Cultivate SEL, Civic Engagement, and a Healthy Democracy by Lauren M. Fullmer, Laura F. Bond, Crystal N. Molyneaux, Samuel J. Nayman, and Maurice J. Elias (#122029)

Teaching the Core Skills of Listening and Speaking by Erik Palmer (#114012)

Total Participation Techniques to Engage Students (Quick Reference Guide) by Pérsida Himmele and William Himmele (#QRG117029)

Total Participation Techniques: Making Every Student an Active Learner, 2nd Edition, by Pérsida Himmele and William Himmele (#117033)

What We Say and How We Say It Matter: Teacher Talk That Improves Student Learning and Behavior by Mike Anderson (#119024)

For up-to-date information about ASCD resources, go to **www.ascd.org.** You can search the complete archives of *Educational Leadership* at **www.ascd.org/el.** To contact us, send an email to member@ascd.org or call 1-800-933-2723 or 703-578-9600.